The Truth About Subliminal Advertising

by
Dr. Jack Haberstroh

Cross Cultural Publications, Inc.

CrossRoads Books

Published by **CROSS CULTURAL PUBLICATIONS, INC.**
CROSS ROADS BOOKS
Post Office Box 506
Notre Dame, Indiana, 46556, U.S.A.
Phone: (219) 272-0889
FAX: (219) 273-5973

©1994 CROSS CULTURAL PUBLICATIONS, INC.
ISBN: 0-940121-17-4
Library of Congress Catalog Card Number: 94-071051

To our son, Phil

June 1, 1958 - November 23, 1991

Table of Contents

Introduction

Introduction

This is a book that should have been written nearly twenty years ago.

Long before the subject of subliminal stimulation swept through the high schools and universities of the U.S. like some fascinating fashion. Long before it became ubiquitous cocktail conversation. And certainly long before 62% of the American public began believing that advertising practitioners are intentionally inserting invisible messages into nearly all the ads and commercials they create.

Yes, almost two-thirds of all American adults are convinced that tens of thousands of advertising agency artists are toiling into the darkest part of the night deliberately placing undetectable objects and words into advertising artwork. Words and objects no one can possibly hear or see. Words like "sex", "fuck", and "cunt." Objects like castrated penises, scorpions, skulls, rats, mice, wolves, tumescent nipples on eager female breasts, and vaginas before and after intercourse. Include also the acts of masturbation, hetero and homo sex, cunnilingus, fellatio, and bestiality with dogs and donkeys.

All this retouching and artistry supposedly sells products and services. Yet, there's no proof worth discussing that inserting anything subliminally in advertising artwork will produce the tiniest increase in sales. Why any advertising professional — or amateur for that matter — would take the time and trouble to embed anything that can't be perceived, is anyone's guess.

Though no one appointed me to be the Official Apologist for the advertising industry, my research clearly suggests agency practitioners aren't embedding a damned thing!

So...

...why in the world do 62% of all American adults think they are?

I've spelled out seven reasons for the myth's popularity in Chapter 7, "<u>Why</u> are there so many believers?" The biggest reason may be the last of the seven, the silence of the advertising business itself.

It's a craft that prides itself on its ability to attract attention to itself and the products it represents. It's principal purpose, of course, is to sell things for its clients. But, strangely, it hasn't been able to shake the murky legend that it's burying a lot of prurient things that can't be heard or seen in its advertising creations.

The reason? It hasn't really tried. Since 1973, when Dr. Wilson Bryan Key's first book, *Subliminal Seduction*, hit book stores like a flaming arrow, the fire's been out of control. A million-seller, it is "must" reading in many college courses. Even an occasional advertising professor will require its reading. It is often assigned to high school health, psychology, and social studies students. Dr. Key's subsequent three books — critics claim he simply rewrote the first book three times — have collectively sold more than a million copies.

In a 1984 4,000-word cover piece in Advertising Age, I scolded my professional advertising colleagues for remaining mute about the phenomenon. They, like I, had said or written little about the phenomenon since it reappeared in whips and leather in 1973. All of us were so sure "it" — like the wanton groupies Dr. Key finds in most ice cube art — would disappear when the ice melts.

Instead, it spread like the pox. Today there's almost as great a percentage of Americans who believe advertising practitioners are embedding subliminals as the percentage of Americans who have brown hair!

But professionals largely ignore it. Advertising Age, the largest circulation advertising publication in the world, has published <u>one</u> article (a review of Dr. Key's fourth book) on the subject in the last five years! and the American Association of Advertising Agencies has been struck dumb.

The result?

You know the result. The strategy of let's all hold our breath, mum's the word, ignore the sonofabitch — and he and his nincompoopery will go away — hasn't worked!

Most well meaning advertising professionals consider it preposterous — beneath them — to even discuss Dr. Key's kinky
claims. My respect for that view has worn thin. Those of us who
teach future advertising professionals have an enormous stake in
the public invalidation of Dr. Key's subliminal theories. Most of
my students hear about subliminal advertising in high school, long
before they reach my classrooms. And they may have discussed the
subject in other university classes in psychology, sociology, art, history, to name a few.

The goal of this small book is to provide the public with the
most accurate information possible on the subject of subliminal
advertising. Namely, it doesn't exist as a practice. It doesn't work.
Advertising professionals are not engaged in it, etc... just some of
the material covered in this small volume.

My professional advertising colleagues and I have remained
silent about it too long.

Author's Note

Author's note

Dr. Key's devotion to the devilment sketched into ice cubes prompted the title of this book. Most of the hidden words and body parts he finds in advertising, he discovers in ice cubes. Even more outlandish, Dr. Key claims that ice cubes can have gender! And therefore sex!

In a Cinzano advertisement one ice cube is male, he claims, using its "long cylindrical shape" to seduce the female cube. It's missing an elliptical shaped chip, or a "portion of the cube's anatomy," Dr. Key contends. That of course, makes that cube female!

Chapter 1

<u>What</u> is it?

Chapter 1

<u>What</u> is it?

Subliminal advertising is advertising beneath the threshold of conscious perception. We can't see it, hear it, or perceive it in any fashion.

The word "subliminal," of course, comes from the fusion of two Latin words: "sub" and "limen." "Sub" meaning "lower than," "beneath," or "under." And "limen" meaning "threshold," an "entrance," or "the point at which one passes into or emerges from."

It is, therefore, the registration of a message within an advertisement, below an individual's conscious perception.

It is "under the line" of conscious discernment. Morse and Stoller define it as:

"any image, word, or sound perceived outside the 'normal range of consciousness.'"

Pratkanis and Aronson put it only slightly differently:

"By <u>subliminal</u> we mean a message so faint or fast that it is presented below the threshold of awareness."

And they add:

"It is a scary world indeed if advertisers can use such a devilish technique to bypass our conscious intellect and beam subliminal commands directly to our subconscious."

Dr. Key, in his first book, *Subliminal Seduction*, discusses the scope of such message manipulation:

"This book acknowledges the role of conscious

perception, but it will concentrate upon <u>unconscious</u> perception — subliminal experiences which manipulate, manage, or control human behavior, but of which humans are consciously unaware. The entire subject of human subliminality is largely unknown, even though omnipresent in the behavioral environment."

I might add that <u>this</u> book will deal largely with commercially persuasive messages (advertising) intentionally aimed at a threshold below human perception (subliminal).

While advertising agencies, research firms, and clients continuously conduct testing concerning the efficacy of <u>supraliminal</u> advertising messages...

...they've never found a single individual switching brands because of a <u>subliminal</u> advertising message! More about this matter in Chapter 4, "Does it work?"

Subliminal advertising messages are communications hidden from view in print, unheard and unseen in broadcast and television. An important point. Research described in Chapter 3, "Does it Exist?" was aimed at advertising agency art directors. I surveyed 100 of them in a nationwide probability sample of large and small agencies. Most of those who responded wrote personal notes about their answers to my questions regarding their possible involvement with subliminals. Their comments often revealed an ignorance — perhaps excusable — about exactly what a subliminal message is. Excusable, because of the lack of experience with subliminal embedding by virtually all of them. But I was surprised, nonetheless. Several thought it was simply sexual suggestion in an advertisement. One or two felt it was "subliminal" to pose a tall, handsome man in the background of an ad for a cologne targeted at young females. Another thought an ad or commercial which revealed considerable female cleavage was "subliminal."

In these examples — cleavage, man in the background, etc. — the "message" is clearly supraliminal. It's there, visible, obvious, and generally undisguised.

Professor Theodore Schulte of the University of Kentucky, raises an interesting point in his Ad Age piece on the subject:

"Color and music are the only known areas
where the subconscious might be influenced in
product choice. The rest is pure, unfounded hog-
wash.."

Color, of course, for most of us is rather clearly perceived. And
music, a marvelously persuasive form of communication, is obviously supraliminal. But what color and music tell our subconscious,
if anything at all, is purely speculative.

For our purposes, there are at least three ways to produce a subliminal advertising communication.

First, flashing a message or illustration on a screen (usually
with a tachistoscope or similar device) so quickly that the viewer is
unaware of it. (E.g. Vicary's 1957 movie theater experiment.)
Secondly, playing an audial message at a subaudial volume level.
At such low volume, usually beneath a "carrier" of music, ocean
waves, etc., that the message cannot be heard. (E.g. Dr. Hal
Becker's "black box" anti-shoplifting device.) Thirdly, etching or
drawing hidden words and objects within larger illustrations. (E.g.
the Gilbey's gin tonic advertisement with the letters "S""E""X" on
each of three of the ice cubes. (Fig. 1)

Some would argue that there are other ways to communicate
subliminally in advertising through suggestion, etc. Distinctions
between subliminal and supraliminal in such instances, however,
fade appreciably.

Chapter 2

<u>Who</u> started it?

Chapter 2

<u>Who</u> started it?

Most researchers date the illicit birth of subliminal persuasion in the United States to the summer of 1957, and the movie theater experiment conducted by James Vicary in Ft. Lee, New Jersey. In fact, it was James Vicary who invented the term: subliminal advertising.

Fascinating individual. Little is known of him, other than his popcorn and Coca-Cola research in the Ft. Lee movie house.

At the time of the experiment, James Vicary was a researcher in his struggling Subliminal Projection Company.

That firm, and many others like it, were moving swiftly into the murky world of motivational research. The world of psychology and psychoanalysis. Into semantics, symbolic logic, sociology and anthropology.

Led by its apostles, Ernest Dichter and Pierre Martineau, marketers all over the map were beginning to use new depth approaches in their work. Beginning in the early 50s, top-drawer clients were beginning to insist that their advertising agencies dig into consumer fears, guilt feelings, hidden needs, and product sexual overtones.

As Jeffrey Trachtenberg puts it in a 1987 Forbes article:

> "Women would pay 25 cents for a bar of soap that made their hands clean, but $2.50 for a bar of soap that promised to make their hands beautiful. Selling plain soap was selling product performance. But add some skin cream and you are selling hope — psychologically more powerful, economically more profitable."

Trachtenberg notes that many of the motivational research tools now being used by Madison Avenue, would have been familiar to Vance Packard — thirty years ago.

Packard's 1957 *Hidden Persuaders* reviews many of the new uses of M.R. It appeared earlier than Vicary's t-scope movie theater stunt. Though Packard didn't discuss subliminal advertising, at least by its new name, his book should have set off consumer alarms all over the country. Consumers would never again feel safe from the motivational researchers who would soon be getting inside their minds, their hearts... and their wallets.

One of Vicary's earlier studies dealt with the eye-blink rate of female shoppers in supermarkets. Our eyes normally blink at approximately 32 blinks per minute. The blink-rate increases to 50 or 60 blinks per minute when we're agitated, or when we get very excited. Vicary trained his cameras on the eyes of shoppers as they entered the supermarket and discovered that as the women shopped, their eye-blink rate dropped...and dropped...to 14 blinks a minute. The women, he noticed, often wore glassy stares, and even bumped into one another. He concluded that the women were in hypnoidal trances!

Another earlier study of his, of mild interest to the apparel industry, found that "psychological spring" lasts five months. "Psychological winter" lasts barely two months.

It was also James Vicary who contended that the experience of a woman baking a cake could be symbolically likened to a woman giving birth. And then presenting the new baby — the cake — to her happy family.

But, by far, his most famous (or notorious) research project was the embedding experiment he conducted in the Ft. Lee, New Jersey theater for six weeks during the summer of 1957.

He mounted a tachistoscope (t-scope) in the projection booth of the theater and flashed two messages on the screen at a speed far too fast to be seen by anyone. The messages were blinked at 1/3,000th of a second, every five seconds, all during the playing of the movie "Picnic." The movie starred a young William Holden and a dazzling blonde, Kim Novak, making her film debut. The two messages were: "Drink Coca-Cola, " and "Hungry? Eat Popcorn."

Vicary later claimed that Coca-Cola sales increased 18.1%. He said popcorn sales jumped 57.8%.

That's about as much as the public remembers about Vicary's famous experiment. What the public has forgotten, or may never have known in the first place, is that Vicary later admitted he had falsified his data. There actually had been no changes in popcorn or Coca-Cola sales as the result of using the flashing hidden messages. When challenged by Henry Link, President of the well-known Psychological Corp., to duplicate his experiment under rigid controls, Vicary accepted the challenge.

He repeated the experiment. No increase in the sale of popcorn or Coke was detectable. Later Vicary recanted and admitted he had lied about the earlier results.

All this was, of course, widely reported in the trade press.

But the mass media scarcely noticed Vicary's recantation. Nor did the public. Instead, newspapers mistakenly vilified Vicary's "successful" experiment along with its "terrifying" t-scope!

Newsday called the t-scope "the most alarming invention since the atomic bomb!" After all, the media speculated, if subliminal messages could sell bags of popcorn and Coca-Colas, what else might they sell? Communism? Devil worship? Perversion? Sin? Who knew?

New Yorker claimed that the minds of Americans had been "broken and entered." Several radio stations began broadcasting subaudible messages, such as "TV's a bore," and "Isn't TV dull?" WAAF in Chicago began offering advertisers subliminal radio commercials. 500 radio commercials no one could hear, for only $1,000, the station boasted.

TV stations got into the act. KTLA in Los Angeles began to air a series of subliminal "Drive safely," and "Don't be a litterbug," messages. With no apparent results. WTWO in Bangor, Maine asked viewers subliminally to write to the station. There was no increase in its mail. And the Canadian Broadcasting Corp. subliminally requested viewers "Telephone now!" No one called.

The FCC at the time expressed its "grave concern." Two laws making subliminal advertising unlawful were introduced in the House of Representative in 1958. Both died in committee. In 1959 another anti-subliminal law was introduced. It also succumbed in committee. How, cooler heads reasoned, could a law be passed regulating something that couldn't be heard, seen, or perceived in any way?

The very notion of subliminal advertising began as a fraud. As an experiment in deceit. All to save the floundering fortunes of a dishonest research firm.

At least one researcher doubts the very existence of Vicary's Ft. Lee theater experiment. Stuart Rogers, a well-known professor of marketing management and communications at the University of Denver, claims the very idea of the subliminal theater experiment was a figment of Vicary's fertile imagination. Reporting in a 1992-93 Public Relations Quarterly, Rogers suggests that Vicary may have been lying avout its existence when he later told reporters about the "scientific test" he had conducted in the Ft. Lee movie house.

The deception may have remained forever buried...

...but for Dr. Wilson Bryan Key.

As this volume goes to press, the ubiquitous Dr. Key is in his late 60s. He misses few American or Canadian college campuses as he continues to maintain a slightly slowing lecture schedule. Auditoriums continue to be packed with enthusiastic, cheering disciples.

He seems to be "preaching to the choir." His head closely shaved to make himself look like "a giant penis" (he once told me), he comes across as fervent, knowledgeable, and very well read. He is also — given his wild and whacky message — quite believable.

His illustrated lectures command $3,000 fees, and at last look, he was giving 20 to 30 of them a year.

He also appears in hundreds of university classrooms every year. And is omnipresent on the TV and radio talk-show circuit. Newspaper and magazine reviews of his books appear frequently.

And his four books have now sold more than 2 million copies.

Subliminal Seduction

His first book, *Subliminal Seduction*, has accounted for nearly half of all sales of books authored by Dr. Key. It appeared in 1973, has now been translated into Spanish, and continues to sell well.

The book is enjoying its seventh printing, and is generally considered the watershed publication on the subject of subliminal advertising.

Marshall McLuhan, with whom Dr. Key taught at Western Ontario University in Canada, gave the book a stem-winding but nonetheless flattering introduction.

The book is, of course, a published monument to theoretical sappiness. It's a volume-long indictment of the mercenary madcaps on Madison Avenue who supposedly fill the advertising they create with hidden messages and symbols which only Dr. Key can find.

In 1974 Dr. Key told me he conducted all of the "research" for *Subliminal Seduction* using his students at Western Ontario University in Canada.

On the first day of class he would have his students lie on the grass and stare at the clouds. And then reveal to Dr. Key the creatures they saw in the clouds. Properly "prepared," on the next day of class they stared at magazine advertisements. And the creatures that lurked in the artwork.

The book opens with their interminable examination of the now infamous Gilbey's tom collins 1971 Time Magazine advertisement. (Fig. 1) The ice cubes, of course, spell out "s-e-x" to Dr. Key. His students meanwhile reported they were feeling aroused, stimulated, sexy, and even "horny." All while staring at a slide of the same tall frosty cocktail.

From this, and other similarly preposterous "research, " Dr. Key concludes:

> "You cannot pick up a newspaper, magazine or pamphlet, hear radio, or view television anywhere in North America without being assaulted subliminally by embeds such as those in the ice cubes.

Incredulous though you might be at this point, these
subliminal SEXes are today an integral part of modern American life — even though they have never
been seen by many people at the conscious level."

Not content with finding just "S-E-X" in the tom collins illustration, Dr. Key also discovers a winking cartoon face in the top ice
cube. It seems to be gazing at the cubes below. A woman's face is
also peering from behind the "X" in the bottom cube. However,
she's looking at the bottle cap, with its "man's legs and partially
erect genitals." Dr. Key promises us much more "to come, if you'll
pardon the expression."

The melting ice beneath the bottle cap is — as you may have
suspected by now — seminal fluid. And the scene, Dr. Key concludes, "is likely after orgasm, not before."

That interpretation, he finds, is reinforced by the less than fully
extended penis in the artwork. There is also seminal fluid distributed all over the bottle of gin. And, between the glass and the bottle, Dr. Key finds vaginal lips and "a drop of water which could represent the clitoris." This "still-open vagina is where the discharged
penis has just been."

Dr. Key also finds at least one other vagina — this one closed
— plus three women and a male voyeur in the top ice cube. The
subliminal reward for breaking out the frosty bottle is "simply a
good old-fashioned sexual orgy!"

"Peer Deeply Into My Ad" Dr. Key asks us in a chapter heading. Yes, into a rather innocuous Esquire advertisement for Coca-
Cola's Sprite. Once again, it's an ice cube in the ad at which he
aims his microscope:

"The right side of the ice cube above the lime
slice forms the back of an animal — a large shaggy
dog with a pointed nose, or quite possibly a polar
bear. The animal's legs are extended outward to the
left, parallel with the top of the lime. The animal's
arms (or legs, as you will) appear to be holding
another figure which is human with long, feminine
hair. Her face is located just above the animal's
head.

The two figures, animal and human, are in what can only be described as a sexual intercourse position. The polar bear, dog, or whatever, is in sexual embrace with a nude woman."

A few pages later he finds a golden skull in (what else?) yet another ice cube, this one chilling a Bacardi on the rocks. And he concludes "that one might richly enjoy dying if well fortified with Bacardi rum."

In a chapter labeled "It's What You Don't See That Sells You," Dr. Key finds that ice cubes can have gender and, of course, sex with each other, as well.

He directs our attention to two ice cubes in a Cinzano aperitif quarter-page in Time Magazine. The ice cube "on the left, of course" is female, he claims. This, because an "elliptical-shaped chip at the top corner of the left-hand ice cube suggests something is missing — a portion of the cube's anatomy!" (underlining mine)

Oh, but there's more. He claims a phallic symbol has been painted into the surface of the cube on the right. Naturally it points directly at the female cube. What's going on between these two cubes?

Need you ask?

Why, they're warming up, of course. The water drops under each one suggest they may be melting. Perhaps getting "hot?" And since more drops appear under the "female" cube, "she" seems to be "warming up faster than the male!" And, what's warming them up? Why, Cinzano, of course!

An innocuous tissue wrapper in a Chivas Regal Scotch advertisement — another inside Time Magazine back cover — is really a dog, "probably a German shepherd or collie," Dr. Key explains. The dog, he declares with no supporting research whatsoever, "appears to provide an unconscious stimulus for the purchase of alcohol."

He claims, in the same passage, that Chivas Regal drinkers will serve this expensive Scotch only to their "very best friends, clients, or special guests whom they are trying to impress." So, Dr. Key, asks, who are the "friends" in the headline who "won't think less of you if you don't serve Chivas Regal?" Why, the tissue-pooch in the ad, of course. But you knew he was going to say that, didn't you?

Perhaps the *Subliminal Seduction* champion, in terms of the variety and number of embeds in a single advertisement, is the Calvert Extra Blended Whiskey full-page which appeared in the October, 1971 issue of Playboy. (Fig. 2).

The eerie menagerie is described on pages 100 through 106. One can only imagine the time it would have taken an artist to paint in the throngs of embeds. The bottom of the glass is, in Dr. Key's view, a volcano — an "ancient symbol of fertility."

And a fish appears "just to the left of the volcano's erupting center." It is, of course, "phallically penetrating the water as it swims." A mouse appears to be riding the fish. And above the mouse's head is the sun, with a skull appearing to its left. On the sun's right, however, is a gaggle of scorpions, with three wolf faces appearing above them. One of the wolves seems to be biting another. The head of a rat is also visible. And there's a lizard "along the glass rim."

Also visible to Dr. Key in the same cocktail is the head of a shark, a white bird, two masks of some kind, a second fish, and a swan under the fish. A pair of human eyes are staring at us from under the swan's neck. There's also a grinning white cat and dozens of embedded S-E-Xs.

Dr. Key admits that the details in the advertisement "must have required hundred of hours of labor by the artist." But he never tells us why or how that labor becomes a cost-effective advertising investment.

Later Dr. Key blithely suggests that Titian, Rembrandt, Picasso, and others embedded words in their art. And the words "produced a strange effect upon art patrons."

What effect the word "fuck", which Dr. Key finds embedded on a doll's arm in a full-page New York Times Sunday Magazine advertisement would have, is anyone's guess. And, just so we won't miss "fuck" on the doll's left arm in the Horsman Doll

Company ad, Dr. Key has that portion of the doll's arm greatly enlarged. (The word can still only be imagined, however, despite the enlarging.) And we are left wondering why in the world a doll manufacturer would consider doing such a thing.

Few symbolic or subliminal details escape Dr. Key's magnifying glass. In an advertisement for the Army Nurse Corps appearing in Cosmopolitan, a smiling female model has been posed in her army fatigues. But, Dr. Key reminds us, a pair of scissors, "the tradition-honored symbol of male castration - protrudes as the symbolic testes of a hidden phallic symbol from her breast pocket."

Dr. Key concludes *Subliminal Seduction* by suggesting that subliminal techniques are known by the CIA and FBI, and may possibly be used for "manipulating subversives" or "converting" governments who disagree with U.S. foreign policy.

And finally this stunner: "It may be reassuring to know that Washington has carefully protected the subliminal technology of mass media so it doesn't fall into the wrong hands."

Oh?

Media Sexploitation

Dr. Key's second treatise on subliminals, *Media Sexploitation*, first appeared in 1976. The book takes *Subliminal Seduction* an unsteady step "forward."

While his first volume deals primarily with subliminals buried in advertising, *Media Sexploitation* claims that many manufacturers, particularly those which fashion women's apparel, are likewise embedding subliminals in products. Even in crackers.

Yes, Ritz crackers.

"Embedded on both sides of each cracker is a mosaic of SEXes," Dr. Key declares. (Fig. 3) Of course, he adds, the number of embeds depend on baking conditions. He claims the molds are scored with the word "SEX," but surprisingly, states that the "SEX patterns vary slightly from cracker to cracker ???"

A little further along in the same chapter he maintains that embedding actually makes the crackers taste better. All because of synesthesia, whereby one sensory response has been stimulated by another (though it be subliminal) in a crossover effect.

He concludes that all of these crunchy SEX embeds, "seen" and "digested" over months and years, may have profound effects on our sex drives - "one of the strongest of human drive systems."

A Bell Telephone bill insert uses a twelve-year old girl as a model on its cover. Dr. Key, of course, finds "SEXes" all over her legs, and the word "fuck" on her stockings.

A one-toothed baby boy is the model in a Crest toothpaste ad appearing in the September 10, 1971 issue of Life Magazine (Fig. 4). The mother of the infant is holding his lower lip down to show a proud father the baby's single tooth. The headline reads: "If you don't take care of this tooth, the permanent one might not be so cute."

But Dr. Key, in a chapter called "Children in the Tit Culture," naturally finds much more. "The mother's phallic forefinger (is) holding down the bottom of the child's open, female-genital symbolic mouth..." On the back of the child's hand appears a series of embedded SEXes (Fig. 4)."

"SEXes are also embedded on the faces of both parents," he claims, "in their hair, on the mother's hand and fingers, and mosaiced across the child's dress."

After several pages of claptrap about the huckstering of detergents using messages directed to our anal-erotic tendencies and fixations, Dr. Key finds a treasure chest of hidden erotica in a 30-second Liquid Plumr TV commercial.

The ever-present "housewife," looking for leaks under her clogged sink, is shown gazing fondly and longingly at the stiff upright drainpipe." Euphoric affection "spreads across her face," Dr. Key notes.

Of course her sink is still half-full of yucky water. Does she grab the Liquid Plumr and toss half of it into the sink? Not to hear Dr. Key tell it.

Instead, "the long cylindrical phallic container with the domed top, is caressingly held in the housewife's delicate fingers as she confidently pours the life-giving fluid, etc., etc." You get the idea.

And again, the professor finds "SEX" in the bubbles of nasty water swirling down the drain. "As an added subliminal feature," he reveals, "a face appeared on the bubble just above the final 'X'. Though the eyes are slightly offset, the nose and tooth-filled smiling mouth was readily apparent. The bubble face, above the 'X', formed the ancient skull-and-crossbones symbol of death."

Watch the models carefully, Dr. Key advises us, in commercials for advertising cleaning products. Watch particularly "the strained body-language positions from which the housewife models mop their floors. Appliances, brooms and mop handles usually point toward genital areas. Often the model has twisted her posture into an absurd contortion to achieve an appropriate genital relationship with her kitchen equipment."

Even the New York Times does not escape Dr. Key's screwy scrutiny. He selects for "analysis" the front page of the Sunday, April 30, 1972 issue A four-column photograph of a helicopter lifting off from a battle scene in Vietnam dominates the top half of the front page. Several ARVN soldiers are desperately clinging to the chopper's landing skids.

Incredibly, Dr. Key finds dozens of SEXes on the soldiers, the helicopter, and the background. This, he says, "to make certain the photo's sales value was increased to the maximum..." "The technique," he theorizes, "does, indeed, sell the news – which sells the advertising which sells the products." And, to prove his point, he cites New York Times net income figures!

"The sexualization of war is hardly a worthy activity," he then moralizes, "even if the end result is increased ad lineage."

Clam-Plate Orgy

This is the third of Dr. Key's four books. It appeared in 1980 and, in addition to the usual discovery of energetic sex organs and objects in advertising, he makes a number of outrageous historical "findings."

The Kraft Soft Parkay Margarine advertisement in a November 1973 issue of Family Circle portrays two penises, he claims. And their castration is punishment for being "old softies."

The ice cubes in a Johnny Walker Black Label Scotch advertisement which ran in many national magazines over a three-year period of time, give Dr. Key the opportunity of locating in them, terrifying faces, dangling legs and arms, a skull, a monster, a turbaned snake charmer, a teddy bear, a one-armed man wearing a Japanese ceremonial mask. And there's much more.

There's a raven, a castrated penis, and a second skull. In sum, Dr. Key claims this single ice cube symbology conjures up nightmarish "hallucinations, self-destruction, even self-immolation." Wonderful way to hype Scotch, right?

He pans one of "the first and most beautiful watercolor landscapes in history." It's a remarkable painting of the great rock at Arco in the Italian Alps (Fig. 5) Albrecht Durer painted the Fenedier Fortified Rock at Arco in 1495. Dr. Key finds at least 33 faces in the magnificent watercolor. One — how he knows this I have no idea — is of a prostitute, another wears a mustache, and several are sleeping.

Even Michelangelo and his magnificent frescoes on the ceiling of the Sistine Chapel are shown little respect. Unseen by millions for more than five centuries, the unfulfilled fellatio in the Original Sin panel is quickly discovered by our extraordinarily perceptive professor. (Figs. 6,7) He tells us that Eve's attempt to excite Adam orally "appears to have been unsuccessful." Her nipples, on the other hand — he so carefully notices — are tumescent, suggesting they are sexually aroused. And few of us would notice in the same panel, as Dr. Key does, a penis-shaped tree branch, complete with testicles. (Fig. 8)

The treasured "Sacred and Profane Love" (Fig. 9) by Titian reveals to Dr. Key that "Profane" is peeping at "Sacred's" genital area. And, curiously, he finds that "Profane" and "Sacred" are really one and the same woman! (Figs. 10,11)

Rembrandt's carefully crafted "Syndics" (Fig. 12), a portrait of six textile merchants of his time, contains several embedded "SEXes," says Dr. Key. Even though the word was spelled "seks, seksual, sekse, and sexe" in idiomatic Dutch of the 17th Century, the embed is quite clearly — at least to Dr. Key — "SEX." Hmmmmm?

Pablo Picasso's 1932 "Woman Asleep: The Dream" (Fig. 13) also does not come away unscathed. The left eye of the sleeping female — oh, why wasn't it obvious to the rest of us? — "forms the coronal ridge at the head of an erect penis." Then we learn from the feverish Dr. Key that she isn't really sleeping after all. She's quietly masturbating.

Perhaps we should forgive the merry mentor for an occasional slip. For an inconsistency between what he claims to see in an illustration at one time, and what he sees in the same illustration at another time.

One occasion, from which the title of his third book grew, occurred shortly after our first meeting in November, 1975. He had given a provocative lecture on subliminal advertising to one of my large advertising classes at San Diego State University.

His first book was already on the market, and selling well. He was working on a second. He was in demand on TV and radio talk shows, and he and his first wife, Iris, seemed to be enjoying life to its fullest.

We went to a long and lively lunch immediately after his guest lecture, and I learned, among other things, that he and I shared a common passion for carefully crafted martinis. At one point he reached into his inside jacket pocket and excitedly withdrew a Howard Johnson's placemat.

He told me that he and his wife had stayed the previous night at the Howard Johnson's Hotel in La Jolla, just north of San Diego. They had had dinner that evening in its adjoining restaurant. "Look at this, Jack," he shouted "just look at this placemat. What does that look like to you, Jack?" And he pointed to the center of the large and colorful placemat.

"Bill," I responded, "looks to me like a porthole...and a bunch of fried shrimp, or clams."

"Oh, c'mon, Jack, hell can't you see <u>it's a vagina and a lot of</u>

pubic hair surrounding it?" he shot back.

"Oh, god, Bill, you can't believe that," I said. And I turned to his charming Irisita and asked her, "do you believe a word of this?" Surprisingly, she answered "not a word, Jack."

The date of the lunch is important. It was November, 1975. *Clam-Plate Orgy* didn't appear until five years later. And I suspect Dr. Key had long forgotten our lunch, and his remark to me about the content of the placemat's illustration.

Instead of a vagina and pubic hair, Dr. Key now claims he found "a donkey astride a human figure." The donkey is licking the stomach of a man with a long mustache. A man and woman, he finds, are busily engaged in oral sex. He discovers at least seven other naked individuals cavorting about in what can only be called a very kinky animal-human sex orgy. A l-o-n-g way from what Dr. Key found on the placemat five years earlier! And, just to make sure we don't miss his latest interpretation, he's outlined in pen each of the individuals and the donkey, on the clam-plate!

Exhausted by the unending panoply of willing vaginas and rigid penises throughout *Clam-Plate Orgy*, many readers may have stopped reading long before its conclusion. That's unfortunate, because Dr. Key reveals much about himself and his political philosophy in the final two pages.

Asked what messages he would subliminally embed in America's media if he wanted to destroy North American society, he responded by saying:

> "U.S. society could be corrupted, disoriented, and very possibly destroyed by doing precisely what the mass media are presently doing with subliminal embedding."

Dr. Key was also asked about the long-term effects of such embedding — say, over a twenty-year period. His response:

> "As to long-term effects, I suggested they simply look out the window. The effects of massive subliminal indoctrination are already highly visible. Large numbers of U.S. children regularly freak out

on every conceivable chemical they can swallow or
pump into their veins. The U.S. family is a disaster
area, with nearly half of all marriages ending in
divorce. American men and women are alienated
and distrustful of each other, their reproductive
behaviors shunted through masturbatory fantasies of
bizarre and unrestrained sexual indulgence. Our
general population is anaesthetized toward reality
by immersion in endless hours of mind-deadening
media pap – a perverse, destructive manipulation
into fantasies of instant gratification, endless sensu-
al indulgences, and purposeless consumption just
for the sake of consumption – and corporate profits."

The Age of Manipulation

John O'Toole, former President of the American Association of
Advertising Agencies, wisely claims Dr. Key has written "the same
book for the fourth time." And, indeed, he has.

The Age of Manipulation appeared in 1989. It is more of the
same. However, if there are degrees of outrageousness, I suspect
this book of Dr. Key's hits new lows.

He finds the Pope engaging in fellatio, with Christ looking on,
in a Chivas Regal magazine advertisement. Another Chivas Regal
ad displays some penis-stroking by another man. The same advertisement shows a "phallic bottle" penetrating the whiskey glass.

Dr. Key finds a McDonald's advertisement revealing a pene-
trated vagina-like dip cup dripping with "symbolic seminal fluid"
from a chicken McNugget.

Betty Crocker's Super Moist cake mix promises to "super-
moisten the housewife's vagina." The icing on the cake, displayed
on the box, is "an accurate tumescent female genital."

Wishbone Salad Dressing has a bottle design, Dr. Key explains,
that includes a "male phallic upper portion and an elliptical female
bottom." In a thirty-second TV spot for the product, a female model
seems to be licking "the female portion of the bottle."

A Tanqueray Gin advertisement "promises subliminally to

improve your erection," Dr. Key asserts. "A formidable, erect, male genital has been embedded into the gin stream," he claims. But then, in the same illustration, Dr. Key finds screaming faces and a lion's head. All, presumably, to assist in selling more of this first-rate gin.

An American Association of Advertising Agencies poster (Fig. 14), mailed by the thousands to U.S. universities and instructors in advertising in the spring of 1986, shows a highball and the head-line: "People have been trying to find the breasts in these ice cubes since 1957." The poster mailing represents the only major, indus-try-wide attempt to educate college and university professors about Dr. Key's kooky concepts. While Dr. Key admits he could find no female breasts in the poster...he did find an erect penis, several grotesque faces, animals of every description, and a shark.

The book goes downhill from there. It is , as Mr. O'Toole so correctly points out, a third rewrite of this now tedious material. Simply more of the same.

Chapter 3

Does it even <u>exist</u>?

Chapter 3

Does it even <u>exist</u>?

As a practice, no. It doesn't exist.

As an epiphenomenon, perhaps.

Subliminal advertising may be a contradiction in terms.

"Sub" "limen" — as we learned in the first chapter — the coupled terms mean "under the line" of conscious perception. Linking the word "subliminal" with "advertising" makes little sense.

Bovee and Arens define advertising as:

> "...the nonpersonal communication of information, usually paid for and usually persuasive in nature, about products (goods and services) or ideas by identified sponsors through various media."

Is any information being communicated at the unconscious or subconscious level? Is it persuasive in nature? Is it about products and services? Are the sponsors clearly identified?

"Nonpersonal" simply means the communication will occur through a medium, and will be directed toward groups of targeted individuals, rather than toward a single person. Certainly we can agree that the movie theater audience, exposed to subliminal messages about CocaCola and popcorn, is a target group. But what information about Coke and popcorn was transmitted? And, assuming the messages were "below the line" of perception, how persuasive were they?

Since we never consciously perceived those communications, how can anyone possibly identify the sponsors of such messages?

As we'll see in Chapter 4, scores of research studies suggest there's no significant market behavior change due to subliminal embeds of any kind. Nor is ad memorability enhanced through their use. "Messages," if one wants to call them that, are not getting through to any target group.

The primary purpose of advertising is to sell something to somebody. A view that finds rather widespread support from many textbook authors, all clients, and even a trade press columnist or two.

David Ogilvy, founder of Ogilvy & Mather, had this to say about the basic purpose of advertising in a recent piece he wrote for The Advertiser. Title of the article, "We sell. Or else.":

> "If I could persuade the creative lunatics to give up their pursuit of awards, I would die happy.
>
> In a survey Ogilvy & Mather recently conducted in several countries, we asked manufacturers what function they want their advertising to perform. The large majority told us they want it to increase their sales.
>
> ...When I write an ad, I don't want you to tell me you find it 'creative.' I want you to find it so persuasive that you buy the product — or buy it more often.
>
> This has been my philosophy for 50 years, and I have never wavered from it, no matter what the temptations have been to jump on the fashionable bandwagons which afflict the ad business."

The purpose of selling is being subverted, of course, if the persuasive message is not perceived. If there is no conscious registration of the communication's perception. If the message is garbled, misunderstood, or unperceived. If the message is, indeed, "subliminal."

The evidence is so slender for anyone having the ability to unconsciously perceive stimuli transmitted subliminally — especially of a persuasive nature — that most researchers, as we'll see, have cast doubts on the efficacy of such transmission.

Baltasar Gracian, a Jesuit scholar and 17th century Spanish

anecdotist, might well have been describing subliminal advertising in his *The Art of Worldly Wisdom: A Pocket Oracle:*

> "Things pass for what they seem, not for what they are."

When Dr. Key asks us to "see" tumescent nipples and rigid penises in advertising art, the results say more about Dr. Key than they do about the respondents. His "research" simply confirms a perception of him as a kook.

When he asks a thousand of his students at the University of Western Ontario (he admitted to me in 1974 that all the "research" he conducted for *Subliminal Seduction* he did using his students there) what they "see" in a Gilbey's gin and tonic advertisement, he's asking the wrong people the wrong question. While Bill Key, the book hustler, may not recognize the difference, Dr William Bryan Key, the social scientist, should.

His "scholarship" is beneath him. It comes closer to perversion than it does to scholarly research.

He asks his students to describe their feelings as they view his array of booze and cigarette advertisements. None, of course, ever find subliminal messages of any kind immediately, he told me in 1974, when I first met him in San Diego. But, with Dr. Key's guidance, all are soon "discovering" the embedded words and genitalia.

The research question, however, is not asking students what they see. But rather, what was deliberately embedded, if anything, by whoever's responsible for the advertising artwork?

People have been "seeing" things for centuries. In clouds, palms, clothing, bushes, tree leaves and tea leaves. Nearly a thousand years ago Aztecs "saw" a reclining young lady in the silhouette of a mountaintop in Central Mexico. They named the 17,342 ft. peak Ixtacihuatl, meaning "sleeping woman."

As recently as July, 1991, a blank billboard on Beyer Blvd. in Chula Vista, California, was attracting as many as 25,000 gawkers a night. People saw, or thought they saw, in the shadows caused by lights on the billboard, the face of nine-year-old Laura Arroyo. Little Laura, a Chula Vista girl, had been abducted and murdered earlier in the month. Her imagined appearance on the all-white bill-board caused traffic jams two miles long on Beyer Blvd. Noisy ice-cream hawkers and food vendors joined the largely Hispanic throng. Sightseers even built a small shrine to Laura at the site.

To relieve the traffic congestion, the outdoor sign company installed new, brighter lights on the billboard. But gawkers insisted the new light patterns formed the image of yet another Chula Vista girl. This one had been murdered five years earlier.

Stephen Fox, in his delightfully written *Mirror Makers*, lands a few haymakers on Dr. Key and his prurient imagination:

> "Another new reform figure by his excesses helped tarnish the credibility of more serious critics of advertising. In a remarkably silly series of books, a journalism professor named Wilson Bryan Key warned consumers of subliminal sexual manipulations by Madison Avenue. It was a new version of *The Hidden Persuaders*, sans peur and sans research. Key claimed to see the word "sex" embedded craftily in Ritz crackers, in Norman Rockwell's first Saturday Evening Post cover in 1917, in almost anything that Key looked at long enough. Sexual embedding, Key declared with a grand sweep, had been used 'in every political campaign of any magnitude in the United States and Canada for at least twenty-five years — if not much, much longer.' The reader might have wondered how he had managed to examine all those campaigns. No contrite advertising artist ever came forward to confess writing in all those three-letter words — because it did not happen, save in the minds of Key and his admirers."

Has anyone ever embedded anything in advertising? Of course. I've listed a number of isolated instances in the first chapter. None were successful — or persuasive — in any way. Is there a creative whackadoodle in the ad agency business out there somewhere right now embedding something (his own name, perhaps?) in a commercial he has just produced? Possibly. I wouldn't bet on it...

...though whackadoodles will always be with us!

Whenever Dr. Key's been asked whether or not he's questioned advertising artists as to whether or not they've embedded anything in their artwork, he invariable complains of a vast "conspiracy of silence!" On one occasion I heard him respond to the question by saying "they're all paid liars. They won't tell the truth. That's what they're paid for, to lie about products."

Yet, it's <u>his</u> responsibility as a social scientist to "prove" that the genitalia, skulls, three-and-four-letter-words, and all the rest, have been intentionally sketched into advertising art.

Rather than tell me he <u>sees</u> the word "SEX" all over both sides of every Ritz cracker, "prove" that Nabisco has deliberately implanted the word on its crackers (Fig. 3). Show me the scored baking drums. Show me the modified conveyor belts which carry the crackers through seven baking processes. Show me Nabisco baking supervisors admitting that they've been putting "SEX" all over the crackers.

I'll get specifically to Ritz crackers, and my research on them, later in this chapter.

First of all, what response do advertising executives, artists, art directors, copywriters, and practitioners generally, make to Dr. Key's daffy accusations?

Unlike Dr. Key's assertion that there's a giant "conspiracy of silence" in which individual advertising practitioners refuse to disclose their involvement in subliminal embedding, most with whom I've communicated — one-to-one — have been very willing to answer my questions about embeds, and Dr. Key.

Two very conscientious students at Southern Illinois University in Carbondale, Catherine A. Bielong and Thomas J. Linden, assisted me with two studies of practitioner involvement in embedding subliminals in advertising art. Without their persistent help both studies would have been impossible to do.

The first survey we executed was of a historical nature.

Dr. Key wrote his first book over a three-year period, from 1969 through 1972. Many of its illustrations were from magazines published in the late 60s. You can imagine the difficulty of tracking down art directors in the 80s who had worked on magazine advertisements published nearly twenty years earlier.

Given the volatile nature of the advertising industry with its job-hopping personnel, the task seemed insurmountable. But Tom and Cathy and I were determined to contact one or more artists or art directors who had actually worked on ads Dr. Key claimed contained subliminals.

Tom and Cathy went at the job like detectives. And their sleuthing paid off.

First of all, they were able to locate the Account Executive who had worked on the Chivas Regal advertisement which Dr. Key writes about in *Subliminal Seduction*. The paper wrapper, as you may never have suspected, is…well, here's the way Dr. Key puts it:

> "Relax and look at the paper wrapper. A light colored triangular shape directly above the base of the bottle neck forms an eye. To the left and slightly above the eye, a fold in the wrapper sticks up forming an ear. The wrapper fold at the extreme right, white-shaded, forms a nose, with a horizontal fold providing the line for a mouth. The area just above the large label, where a light appears to be glowing, would be roughly the area of the dog's neck. A dog, probably a German shepherd or collie, is the subliminal *modus operandi* of the Chivas Regal advertisement in Time. The ad must work extremely well, as it was frequently reprinted in other publications, such as the New York Times, for well over a year."

Yes, a dog, a German shepherd or a collie, Dr. Key reminds us, has been intentionally embedded in the expensive advertisement. How such a creature will contribute to increased Chivas Regal sales we're never told.

But he does remind us that the ad worked "extremely well," no doubt due to the dog's head tissue wrapper???

Doyle Dane Bernbach, Inc. produced the advertisement, and many more for the same client going back over almost two decades.

The Account Executive at the time was Martin H. Kreston who, by March, 1981, had been promoted to Group Senior Vice President at the agency.

Interestingly, Kreston was also the Account Executive on the "subliminal champion," the 1971 Playboy advertisement for Calvert Extra Dry Whiskey. We called it the "champion" because Dr. Key simply outdid himself in finding more embeds in this single advertisement than in any other: a volcano, a fish, a mouse riding the fish, the sun, a skull, scorpions, three wolf faces, another wolf biting the first wolf, the head of a rat, a lizard, the head of a shark, a white bird, a white mask, another mask, another fish, a swan, a pair of eyes under the swan's neck, a white cat, and dozens of "SEXes." (Fig. 2)

Here's what Kreston wrote to Cathy on March 16, 1981:

> "I am familiar with Dr. Key's book, *Subliminal Seduction.*
>
> I have handled the Seagram account, including Chivas Regal and Calvert Extra, at Doyle, Dane Bernbach since July of 1962.
>
> Dr. Key's claims regarding subliminal activity in the Chivas Regal and Calvert Extra advertisements are apparently his own invention. This agency has never used subliminal advertising. As a matter of fact, there is no evidence that subliminal advertising techniques are being used in this country's advertising, or have been used in this country's advertising. We cannot understand why anyone would want to use a subliminal message of a dog's head, or sexually explicit scenes, to advertise either these products or any other products.
>
> There is no evidence I know of that has ever been presented to substantiate Dr. Key's claims regarding his accusations of subliminal advertising. I can assure you, having been intimately involved in both these advertisements, that Dr. Key's claims are without any foundation whatsoever.

Dr. Key's fevered fantasies reach a new level of looniness in the embeds he finds in the Cinzano Apértif Time Magazine advertisement. He describes his "discoveries" in *Subliminal Seduction*. Dr. Key writes:

"In the Cinzano cubes the artist has included subtle cues which will lead the reader, at both the conscious and unconscious levels, to interpret male or female genital symbols, breasts, nude couples, animals — the possibilities are endless. Cinzano probably really doesn't care what meanings projected into the cubes as long as it attracts the reader's attention and holds his eye on the ad as long as possible so the subliminal sell can take effect.

...Linguistically, gender is not consciously used anymore in English, though masculine and feminine nouns are an important part of Latin-derived languages — Spanish, French, Italian, and Portuguese. Nevertheless, even among English-speaking peoples who do not specifically use gender, sex is vitally important as we label and describe objects in our unconscious. Why not ice cubes?

Thinking in terms of male and female, which of the two Cinzano ice cubes would be female? The one on the left, of course; at least it was so designated by over 90 percent of a thousand test subjects. The elliptical-shaped chip at the top corner of the left-hand ice cube suggests something is missing — a portion of the cube's anatomy. The cube on the right is therefore masculine. Observe the top area of the right-hand cube. A phallic symbol has been painted into the surface. The long, cylindrical shape points directly at the chip in the cube on the left.

...Now ask, what is going on between this female and male set of ice cubes? The drops of water or melted ice, actually painted by an artist, suggest the cubes are melting or warming up. More drops appear beneath the female cube than beneath the male. Obviously, the female is warming up faster than the male.

And how did the ice cubes get turned on? Cinzano, of course."

The advertisement was created by Della Femina, Travisano & Partners, Inc. Ron Travisano could not recall that specific ad in his reply, but did have a few choice words for Dr. Key and his accusations:

"In reply to your letter to me dated February 9th, I don't know the advertisement you're referring to, but it really doesn't matter. If it was an ad done in this agency, the charges Dr. Key makes are ridiculous. We never have and never will do advertising that stoops to that level of taste or stupidity.

The purpose of this agency is to create intelligent and tasteful advertising that reaches or surpasses our clients' goals and, at the same time, nurtures and rewards everyone in this organization.

I would love to have the opportunity to take this thing further, either in person or by mail. I spend much of my time teaching advertising communications and I am appalled at the level at which Dr. Key works. Where is his mind, that he sees sexual fantasies in ice cubes? He's got to be kidding! I guess that's the way he gets his rocks off...so to speak."

Dr. Key sees a beheading in a Johnnie Walker Scotch advertisement placed in The New Yorker, Time, Playboy, etc. Of course you have to turn the ad on its side and look closely to see the "bravely smiling" man — complete with mustache and goatee — being decapitated.

When Tom wrote to Needham, Harper & Steers, the creators of the advertisement, Barry Diederman, President of NH&S, a division of Needham, Harper & Steers Advertising wrote back:

"I haven't read Dr. Key's book, so I'll assume your summary of his comments about that Johnnie Walker ad are accurate.

1. Without seeing the ad in question, I have no idea whether it came out of our office.

2. If it did, I can remember no one in the Creative Department who would have been capable of the lunatic thinking the good doctor describes.

3. At no time in my career, which goes back 25 years, have I ever encountered any copywriter or art director who would have consciously (or unconsciously, for that matter) perpetrated the sexual skullduggery described in your letter.

Maybe "sexploitation," like beauty, is in the eye of the beholder."

A mother is showing off her daughter's first tooth in a Crest advertisement which first appeared in Life Magazine on September 10, 1971. (Fig. 4) The headline admonishes: "If you don't take care of this tooth, the permanent one might not be so cute." The infant's father looks on admiringly. But...what does Dr. Key see?

For openers, the "one-toothed baby in white is, of course, a boy — a pink dress would have meant a girl." (As if baby girls are never dressed in white?) "This ad," he claims, "is a superb example of a subliminal oral-regression persuasion technique."

"When dealt with at the conscious level, the overt genital symbolism is obvious and annoying; the mother's phallic forefinger holding down the bottom lip of the child's open, female-genital symbolic mouth, provides the photograph's primary focal point. For most readers, the fovea in the eye's retina saccades from the open mouth and finger up to the father's face (the curve lines retouched into his cheek), then directly left into the mother's eyes, diagonally down from her nose across the baby's face, down to his (her!) arm and hand, then a quick jump to the left and you see the Crest toothpaste tube.

Now, let's go back and look at what was perceived on the periphery of the retina's fovea, during the lightning-quick conscious perceptual experience.

On the back of the child's hand appears a series of embedded SEXes. (Fig. 4) SEXes are also embedded on the faces of both parents, in their hair, on the mother's hand and fingers, and mosaiced across the child's dress.

Just think about all that Crest has to offer in addition to 'No Cavities.'"

Tom followed up with the advertising agency, Benton & Bowles, Inc. which created the lovable advertisement. And we received a response from The Procter & Gamble Company, manufacturers of Crest, as well.

The Benton & Bowles letter was written by the brand's Assistant Account Executive at the time, Michael Edmeades:

"Thank you for your letter dated April 4, 1981 which referred to claims made by Dr. Key in his book Media Sexploitation, regarding a 1971 Crest ad.

We can assure you that there is no foundation whatsoever to Dr. Key's allegations. The overall objective of the ad is to communicate the importance of forming good habits of oral hygiene at an early age. The ad utilizes a visual of a baby and her ("her!") parents to emphasize how early this practice should begin. The mother is holding down the baby's bottom lip to reveal the baby's first tooth, which is the only way the tooth can be photographed. The intent of the visual is to create an atmosphere of parental love and concern for the well-being of the child. We can find no substantiation for Dr. Key's observations regarding this visual which we feel are totally inaccurate.

Furthermore, there are no S-E-X's embedded anywhere in the ad or any other attempts at subliminal persuasion.

We hope this satisfies your inquiries. If you have any further questions, please advise."

Procter & Gamble's Supervisor of Public Relations, Stuart M. Kunkler, also denied Dr. Key's accusations:

"Your letter to Mr. Levy was referred to me because this falls into my area of responsibility.

Let me assure you that the charges against a Crest toothpaste advertisement in the book Media Sexploitation are absolutely untrue. In the advertisement, the mother is simply exposing her child's first tooth, much as any parent would do. Also, there was no attempt to embed subliminal messages into the advertisement.

Mr. Linden, we believe the First Amendment to the Constitution allows an author the right to express his commentary on our advertising, no matter how bizarre this commentary may be. We can in no way verify Dr. Key's claims.

Thank you for contacting Procter & Gamble, and good luck with your studies."

Other personal letters poured in from professionals, invariably expressing their revulsion for Dr. Key and his claptrap. This one from Stavros Cosmopulos, Creative Director and Chairman of the Board of Cosmopulos, Crowley & Daly, Inc. in Boston:

"...In all the years that I have been on the creative side of this business I've never used subliminal anything in ads. Although I remember an illustrator tried to slip something through once (he got chewed out and was never used again). You are right, the matter does need airing out."

Jeffrey L. Atlas, a Senior Copywriter at Ogilvy & Mather in New York, obviously very upset, wrote:

"For years, I have been infuriated by Mr. Key's charges of 'subliminal seduction.'

I was pleased to read in Advertising Age that someone is attacking these absurd, unfounded, and unsubstantiated lies.

I hope that my revulsion at his charges is apparent.

...It is an insult to everyone in this business that people believe his lies. Of course, the real question is, why do so many believe them?"

His question, of course, is an excellent one. And will be addressed in another chapter of this book.

The Director of Corporate Relations, Charles I. Johanns, of the Kemper Group wrote:

"You deserve commendation for the research you have done into subliminal advertising.

...Your work reveals his books for what they are — rubbish that exemplifies the intellectual bankruptcy of some academics."

Award-winning Diane Cook-Tench, a former Senior Vice President/Creative Supervisor with The Martin Agency in Richmond, Virginia wrote this recent note:

"The idea that professionals in the advertising industry spend time figuring out how to put subliminal messages into ads for their clients is simply silly.

For starters, it presupposes some kind of belief in the effectiveness of subliminal messages; a belief which is not embraced by any professionals I have known in my sixteen years as a working art director and creative supervisor.

It also disregards the massive amount of

research and testing that takes place with consumer groups before ad campaigns are developed and after they're run.

For the most part, clients and agencies work hard to maintain honest, aboveboard relations and communications with the public. Companies investing hundreds of thousands to millions of dollars in their branded products wouldn't gamble that kind of investment on cheap tricks that will only annoy their targeted consumer groups.

The goal of any good advertising is to establish a 'friendship' between the product and the appropriate consumers. To do this well takes all the time and energy professionals possess."

Keith McKerracher, former President of the Institute of Canadian Advertising (the 4As of Canada), called subliminal advertising a "Modern Day Myth" in a 4As February/March 1985 Washington D.C. newsletter.

Jerry Goodis, longtime Canadian advertising practitioner, takes Dr. Key's allegation as "personal insults":

"If anyone in my organization was 'embedding' secret messages in our ads, I would certainly be aware of it. But what I must ask is this: what could possibly be the point of anyone inserting words like 'sex,' death's heads, earthy verbs, euphemisms for female fixtures, or artificially concocted scenes of wanton bestiality into their ads? What possible financial gain would any sponsor hope to glean from the exhortation alleged by Key to be embedded in Time's portrait of Queen Elizabeth, urging everyone to rush out and fornicate?

...It is noteworthy that Key is usually the only person able to see all these hidden messages. And even then, if I understand him, he is only able to do so by relaxing and letting his subconscious mind take command. The rest of us are obviously just too uptight and repressed, too brainwashed by the

Machiavellian media and their lackeys, to see what to Key is exceedingly clear.

It astounds me that it has taken this long for someone to throw down the gauntlet to Wilson Bryan Key and expose his sick, perverted ideas.

What is even more disturbing than Key's infatuation with these ludicrous theories is that some misguided cynics actually believe them. And *that* really scares me."

In a January 30, 1984 Advertising Age, J.J. Johnston, Chairman of the Jim Johnston Advertising Agency in New York, wrote about the existence of subliminal advertising:

"As a creative director who has been at the craft for 20 years, I can assure Mr. Rainer that his belief in subliminal persuasion as a tool of advertising makes as much sense as believing in the Tooth Fairy or the Easter Bunny.

...Quite frankly, I have yet to meet any creative in the advertising business — creative director, writer, art director, designer, tv producer, et al — who has any interest in, let alone used, subliminal persuasion techniques.

Neither have I met any with interest in tachistoscope testing, 'black box' magic, or other such devices. The creative community believes all such academic diversions are humbuggery, and hardly germane to the continuing tough problem of reaching and persuading real people."

In 1984-85 I was invited to appear on approximately forty radio call-in talk shows. The subject, of course, was subliminal advertising — or more specifically the research I supervised which strongly suggests it doesn't exist as a Madison Avenue practice. On two occasions radio show producers volunteered their personal views about embedding subliminals in commercials.

Dick Price, a veteran producer at KARN in Little Rock,

Arkansas, told me in late December of 1984, that he had produced "thousands of radio and television commercials." He then said he "couldn't imagine embedding anything in any of them."

Scott Cassidy of WTKN in Pittsburgh, said essentially the same thing. He claimed he had assisted in the producing of thousands of radio commercials. And he said he "had never seen anyone involved in radio production embedding anything!"

Former Ogilvy & Mather Chairman of the Board, Jock Elliott, wrote to Ad Age about the existence of subliminal advertising:

> "Every time we practitioners visit a campus (which is pretty often), we are almost invariably asked about subliminal advertising. Our continual explanations that the practice simply doesn't exist etc."

Don J. Folger of Fahlgren & Swink in Marion, Ohio also wrote in Ad Age:

> "My distress centers on the silliness of the situation to any advertising professional (describing subliminal embedding). Perhaps that's the reason we don't pay more attention to the academia nuts. Most of us are too busy trying to do a good job for our clients to waste time dignifying a hollow charge with an answer."

Charles B. Jones, head of his own advertising management consultancy in Chicago, described Dr. Key's writings as "patently spurious" in yet another Ad Age letter.

Walter Weir, honored as one of the country's top ten advertising copywriters by Printer's Ink, was recently named a distinguished fellow by the American Academy of Advertising. The author of three books on advertising, he was a copywriter and creative director on Madison Avenue for more than thirty years. "Of course subliminal advertising doesn't exist...but the problem is so many individuals believe it does," he told me in March of 1992. "I thought it was going to go away, but I can see it isn't," he added.

He also revealed that he had acted as a spokesperson for the

Copy Research Council of New York. Some thirty top advertising executives belonged to the loose-knit Council which Weir founded. In 1957 he challenged Vicary to replicate his movie theater experiment. "If you do, Jim," he told Vicary, "you'll be the toast of Madison Avenue!" Weir, who at that time headed his own advertising agency, now operates a Communications consultancy from his home in Newton, Pennsylvania. He has just completed work on his fourth book, published this year by The Haworth Press: *How to Create Interest-Evoking, Sales-Inducing, Non-Irritating Advertising.*

In a 1982 personal letter to Dr. Key, Weir claims he bought Dr. Key's books because of questions asked him about subliminal advertising when he joined the faculty at Temple University:

> "...I read all three and found them masterpieces of inference and implication as well as assumption. In not one did I find one shred of reliable evidence of what you claim is and has been done in advertising — so-called subliminal seduction."

Writing in Ad Age in October, 1984, Weir asserts:

> "Mr. Key's books offer no evidence that subliminal advertising exists or is practiced as widely as he claims. If subliminal advertising did exist, there certainly would be textbooks available on how to practice it. There would be many articles in Ad Age on the subject and countless news items about subliminal campaigns.
>
> There are no secrets in advertising. The only evidence — if it can be called that — Mr. Key presents is his own doctored photographs showing, for example, the letters S, E and X appearing in ice cubes in a drink and a photograph of a plate of fried clams, with the clams outlined by Mr. Key, presumably carefully piled on the plate to represent a sex orgy. How either of these could induce people to buy a brand of liquor or order fried clams, Mr. Key never makes clear."

In *Subliminal Seduction* Dr. Key suggests that Kent cigarettes

were so named because Kent " is a strong masculine name" and the
brand was designed to appeal to women. But, practicing warp-
think, Dr. Key would have us believe that symbolically changing
the "e" in Kent to a "u" — the brand becomes the phonetic slang
term for the female genital — and the cigarettes take on a new
appeal to males.

Walter Weir, however, reminds us in Ad Age that:

> "...Kent cigarets were named after Herbert
> Kent, president of Lorillard at the time the cigarettes
> were introduced."

In one of the very few articles on the subject of subliminal
advertising to appear in Ad Age in the last five years, John O'Toole,
President of the 4As, reviews Dr. Key's 1988 book, *The Age of
Manipulation*. In the review O'Toole makes this observation about
Dr. Key:

> "He probes an ad for Kent cigarettes that I was
> involved with through every step of the creative and
> production processes and asserts that we deliberate-
> ly 'embedded' the word 'sex' in the male model's
> hair. He finds retouching we never did and motiva-
> tions in posing the model that I hope my daughters
> don't read."

Weir also finds interest in subliminal advertising undiminished:

> "Wherever I have lectured or evaluated a course,
> one of the first questions I am asked — by profes-
> sors and students — is how subliminal advertising is
> created. While I do my best to explain why it does
> not exist and could not, the sensationalism of Mr.
> Key's books leaves a mental impression that is dif-
> ficult to expunge."

He then adds this final note:

> "If Mr. Key is so certain of the existence of sub-
> liminal implants, he might be challenged to point
> some out in current advertising so that...Mr. Key's
> (claims) also could be checked."

Dan Jaffee, a former senior vice-president for government relations of the American Advertising Federation in Washington, D.C., takes issue with Dr. Key in an American Bar Association Journal article. His conclusion:

> "There is no evidence subliminal advertising exists."

In September, 1981, the U.S. Bureau of Alcohol, Tobacco and Firearms proposed regulations prohibiting subliminal advertising in the advertising of alcoholic beverages. Chief lobbyist for the American Association of Advertising Agencies and the Director of its Washington, D.C. office, Charles Adams, testified before the BATF. "Does it exist?" he asked rhetorically. "Have there ever been hidden messages in advertising? Yes," he said, "there have been, but the known attempts at subliminal advertising have been both trivial and transitory."

Later in his testimony he asked the question: "Does it currently exist?" His answer:

> "We are quite sure it does not. As far as we know, it has never been used by any of our 5,300 member agencies over the some thirty years since it became a publicized phenomenon.
>
> In my own career in the advertising agency business, I have worked personally with hundreds of advertisers on thousands of advertising campaigns. In not one instance have I ever heard a suggestion — either from an advertiser or an agency person — that any subliminal technique be used. And I have checked this experience with many of my colleagues in the agency business — all of whom agree. Our clients always wanted their advertising to be as liminal as possible."

Earlier in this chapter I suggested that the real research question is <u>not</u> to ask individuals what they <u>see</u> in advertising, but <u>what's been embedded there</u> intentionally?

And our research in the early 80s at Southern Illinois University concentrated on the "doers" — the artists, art directors, etc. — who were in a position (if they had wanted to) to embed subliminals. Our first survey dealt with those who might have embedded something in advertisements which Dr. Key uses as examples in his books, of ads in which he claims messages and objects were embedded. Most of his examples were from the late 60s and early 70s.

But we also wondered about the present-day practice of advertising. Would advertising agency art directors, for instance, who are working on current advertising, admit their involvement in embedding anything?

We selected every 60th advertising agency from the latest Standard Directory of Advertising Agencies (the "red book"), 100 in all.

We put together a brief questionnaire, tested if for understanding, and mailed it, an explanatory letter, and a return-reply envelope, to the art director at each of the selected agencies.

We received 47 usable returns, or 47%. Surprisingly, eight were from agency presidents or owners, three were from creative directors, one from a vice president/graphics, and the other 35 from art directors.

Here are the questions we asked, and their responses:

Question No. 1: Have you ever deliberately embedded a subliminal message (i.e. a word, symbol, or sexual organ not perceived at the conscious level) in advertising artwork for a client?

Response	%	(N)
"No"	96	45
"Yes"	4	2
"No opinion	0	0
	100	47

Question No. 2: Have you ever supervised the embedding of a subliminal message in advertising artwork for a client?

Response	%	(N)
"No"	94	44
"Yes"	4	2
"No opinion"	2	1
	100	47

Question No. 3: Do you have personal knowledge of any <u>other</u> individual who has embedded a subliminal message in advertising artwork for a client?

Response	%	(N)
"No"	92	43
"Yes"	6	3
"No opinion"	2	1
	100	47

Question No. 4: What percentage of advertising agency artwork executed for clients do you feel contains deliberately embedded subliminal messages?

Response	%	(N)
0% to 85%	85	40
Left Blank, or	15	7
"No idea"	0	0
	100	47

The two individuals who responded positively to the first and second questions wrote comments on their returned questionnaires. One said, "all advertising is a mixture of product and subliminal messages, i.e. a product with an attractive person means if you use the product, subliminally you can look like this, feel like this, or receive a positive response from people." The other respondent, an art director from New Jersey, said simply: "Sex sells — whether consciously or unconsciously conceived by an art director or an account executive, etc."

Clearly, neither understood the meaning of "subliminal advertising."

The majority of those surveyed, however, wrote on the margins

of the questionnaire. Invariably they disagreed with Dr. Key that
agency practitioners were adding subliminal messages of any kind
to the artwork.

The following were typical of their comments:

"Any art director on my staff who has time to do
this isn't doing a good job of art direction. I'd fire
his ass!"

"This agency would never be a party to any
advertising of this nature."

"I believe a lot of these claims are exaggerated
or contrived by the viewer. You can even see such
things in clouds if your imagination is good."

"I would welcome Dr. Key to come to our
agency and try to produce an ad that will sell the
client's product, complete with attention-getting
headline, informative body copy, a sound and mem-
orable tag line, and sufficient client identification to
get a better than 50% Starch noted score PLUS put
in some nicely contrived word, symbol, or sexual
organ for a subliminal message...all within budget!
If he can do so, have him give me a call and I'll hire
him at any salary he names."

"Next Key will claim that coffee companies are
hiding messages at the bottom of the pot, or that the
Pentagon is influencing the shape of clouds! I
applaud your study. In the 11 years I spent at Avon
and Revlon as well as some of the most prestigious
New York agencies, I have never heard or seen anything approximating Key's claims."

"If any is done, which I doubt, it would most
certainly be done on a subconscious level. I believe
Dr. Key is on a witch hunt...and is obviously selling
books."

"At our agency we're too busy trying to sell our
client's products. We don't have time to play

games."

"I may be incredibly naive, but in my 20 years in the ad business in San Francisco and L.A., I have never heard of anyone even joking about the above subject."

"My own moral values would not allow me to use sexual sublimination in my work. If a client wanted me to do so, he or she would immediately become an ex-client."

Does subliminal advertising exist? As I said earlier, I consider it a contradiction in terms. No. Certainly not. Scores, perhaps hundreds of practitioners have voiced their outrage in the trade press, personal letters to me and others, on talk shows, etc. Many denunciations of Dr. Key and his psycho-sexual humbuggery have even found their way into Dr. Key's books themselves.

They're all "paid liars," he claims. "The most defensive occupational groups have been print journalists, university psychologists, and physicians," he writes in *The Clam-Plate Orgy*. "I am often amused at the extreme hostility, even open aggression, advertising people display towards my books. They vehemently deny that anything I wrote was true..."

John S. Crosbie, President of the Magazine Association of Canada, calls Dr. Key an "emotionally disturbed...and sick man" in *The Clam-Plate Orgy.*

Other comments were cited in the same book:

From the Vice President & Account Supervisor at Doyle, Dane Bernbach, Inc.:

"Mr. Key's dissection of the 1971 Calvert Extra ad (Fig. 2) may epitomize the delusions of a disturbed personality. Anyone who has looked at Rohrschalk (sic) test or cloud formations knows that perception varies from person-to-person and generally the more neurotic the individual, the more devious the interpretation. Key's book evoked nothing but laughter among those of us at the agency who were involved in that particular ad...it would amuse me if any other agencies or advertisers employed this device. We would never jeopardize our reputation or integrity by dishonest and devious advertising methods."

From the Director of Public Affairs and the Senior Vice President and Research Director of Batten, Barton, Durstine & Osborn, Inc.:

"Subliminal techniques including subliminal stimulation are not used by this agency — or any other competent agency. To waste time considering trying to create a subliminal message that will overcome the intended message would be counter-productive in time and effectiveness... The technique is not used because (a) it has not been proven to be effective; (b) there is some question as to the validity of the technique; (c) we do not see any reason to use advertising techniques such as these."

From the Senior Vice President and Executive Creative Director of Foote, Cone & Belding (at that time the world's fifth largest advertising agency):

"I have read Key's book...and consider it to be a total crock. Subliminal seduction is not used by FC&B because it is dirty, devious, and shows a total lack of respect for the people we ultimately work for — those being consumers of the products we represent. I despise the whole idea of subliminal stimulation."

From the Publicity Director of McCann-Erickson, Inc.:

"We do not subscribe to hidden or devious methods of manipulating consumer behavior, nor do we feel that anyone in the advertising business could do it, even if they wanted to. To believe that it can be done, regularly, on a commercial basis, is to underestimate and disrespect the consumer."

From an account executive at Ross Roy of New York, Inc.:

"It's virtually impossible to implement through photography. And very few people would recognize it even if one could implement it, which would make it quite cost-inefficient and therefore useless."

From the Vice President of Media Research at Leo Burnett:

"...there has been only one 'test' of the subliminal mode of presentation...upon the sale of coke and popcorn to movie-goers. This report (by James Vicary) is now considered as much a hoax as the doctored remains of pre-historic man routinely discovered during the latter half of the 19th century. Vicary was discredited by the market research community and has dropped completely out of sight."

From the Virginia Slims account executive at Leo Burnett:

"Subliminal stimulation is not purposely used by the Leo Burnett Co. in the development of Virginia Slims advertising. The reason is we are advertisers, not psychologists. Our expertise is in the communication of ideas and images, not in the probing of stimulation of the subconscious."

There are, as Dr. Key suggests, at least three possible conclusions to be drawn from this torrent of denial by the advertising industry that it is, indeed, using subliminal techniques.

First, of course, is that the hundreds of advertising executives from scores of agencies — including those Dr. Key himself quotes — are actually telling the truth! And subliminal advertising is nothing more than sexual fantasy, whipped into frothy reality by Dr. Key's turbulent testicular imagination.

Secondly, perhaps all these advertising, public relations, and production executives know nothing about subliminal embedding occurring in their own shops. Hardly. Difficult to believe when one imagines how many hours, for instance, it would take an artist to embed the thousands of "things" which Dr. Key found in a single Calvert Extra Dry Whiskey ad in a 1971 Playboy. (Fig. 2) One can only guess at the enormous price tag — and the screams of rage from the client — for such merrymaking.

Third, he claims, there is always the possibility that subliminals "do not really affect human behavior."

That point we shall explore in the next chapter.

But before leaving the question of the existence of subliminal advertising, let's pause to examine one of the more bizarre accusations Dr. Key makes in his entire quartet of books.

If there can be degrees of whackery, perhaps Dr. Key's whackiest allegation can be found on page 10 of *Media Sexploitation* in a chapter about Ritz crackers called "SEX Can Also Be Crunchy."

> "Take half a dozen crackers out of the box and line them up on the table, face upward. Now relax, and let your eyes linger on each cracker — one at a time. Do not strain to see the surface, however. Usually in about ten seconds, you will perceive the message. Embedded on both sides of each cracker is a mosaic of SEXes. (see Fig. 3)
>
> The number and precise location of each SEX embed appear to depend upon the temperature and time during which each cracker was baked. The SEXes are apparently embedded in the molds pressing out the dough. When baked, the SEX patterns vary slightly from cracker to cracker.
>
> There is probably nothing uniquely evil about using SEX mosaics on soda crackers. In all fairness, embedding really makes the damned things taste better."

This book concerns itself primarily with subliminal advertising. Whether the word "SEX" all over both sides of every Ritz cracker is advertising or not, I'll let the reader decide. One gets the impression that Dr. Key has never seen Ritz crackers being baked. If, for instance, each cracker mold were scored with"SEX" as Dr. Key suggests, the "SEX" pattern would not vary much from cracker to cracker,

The fact is, Dr. Key hasn't the haziest notion how Ritz crackers are produced. Even granting someone could score every single top-of-the-cracker mold in each of the seven widely scattered Nabisco bakeries that make Ritz crackers — over a thousand individual molds — how would all these SEXes he sees appear on the <u>bottom</u> of each cracker?

To find out how Ritz crackers are created, I visited the largest bakery in the world, Nabisco's, at 73rd and Kedzie, on the south side of Chicago. The facility was immaculate. To visualize the Ritz cracker baking process, imagine you are standing on the goal line of a regulation size football field. The process starts on your goal line, and ends some 300 feet away. On your goal line is a giant hopper consuming a steady stream of grayish dough flowing into it from two conveyor belts. Two heavily muscled men stand above the hopper and push the dough down into its gaping interior with large paddles. The dough is squeezed against a rotating drum, roughly four feet in diameter, on which there are six rows of cracker molds, ten across. The drum revolves rapidly and a "reciprocating wire" cuts ten crackers off at a time, dropping them gently onto a moving conveyor belt.

The conveyor belt then takes them on a straight line through seven individual baking processes. Finally, the crackers are oiled and salted, some 300 feet from the hopper where it all began. The crackers then move to another floor where they are wrapped and boxed.

This one location produces 108,000 boxes of Ritz crackers every day! 71,280,000 crackers from this single bakery every week!

Supervisors permitted me to get within a foot of the spinning drum with its molds. I could see the cracker molds clearly immediately after the soft crackers had left the drum. None of the molds were scratched or scored. I also scrutinized the conveyor belt on which — every second or so — ten crackers were gently placed. Spotlessly clean, the conveyor belt was free of any words or objects whatsoever.

The baking supervisor on that floor told me he had heard about Dr. Key's accusations. He laughed derisively at the entire notion of embedding anything in the crackers. "The most difficult thing we have to do is keep them all the same color," he told me.

Caroline Fee, Manager of Corporate Communications at Nabisco Brands Inc. in Parsippany, New Jersey, explained the Ritz cracker baking process in a June, 1992 letter to me. To the best of her knowledge, the baking process had not changed appreciably since my 1985 visit. Here's her letter:

"Nabisco makes millions of Ritz crackers each day in several bakeries throughout the country. The dough is cut out to form the crackers by giant metal rolls that continuously revolve over the cracker dough. One revolution of this drum cuts 60 crackers. The same drum revolves again and again to cut out the millions of crackers made each day. A standardized drum is used in all our bakeries making it impossible for each cracker to have a different pattern as it is cut.

As the cracker bakes, the bottom conforms to the surface on which it is baked. It is not possible to imprint a pattern on the bottom of a baked good such as this. The markings to which Dr. Key refers are simply the bubbles which form in the cracker dough as it is baking. As the dough bubbles, the raised spots cook a little more because they are closer to the heat source. As each unbaked cracker rises in a slightly different way, it is understandable that each cracker could look somewhat different.

We cannot understand how Dr. Key arrived at his theories about Ritz crackers. We find it unbelievable that he could make these suggestions had he ever see the cracker production process. We appreciate the opportunity to respond to your questions about Ritz and hope this clarifies our position."

Chapter 4

Does it <u>work</u>?

Chapter 4

Does it <u>work</u>?

No, it doesn't.

Of the scores of research studies on the effectiveness of sub-liminal advertising in a market environment, only two or three sug-gest subliminals work. And those studies have been invalidated by later, more thorough, research.

Subliminal advertising does not affect consumer buying behav-ior, advertising recall, or any other marketplace behavior. Which, of course, prompts the obvious question: why in the world would any advertiser, or ad agency, think about using it?

Here's the way the authors of the excellent *Age of Propaganda* put it:

> "During the last few years, we have been col-lecting published articles on subliminal processes, gathering more than 150 articles from the mass media and more than 200 academic papers on the topic (a stack nearly 2 feet tall).
>
> In <u>none of these papers</u> is there clear evidence in support of the proposition that subliminal messages influence behavior. Many of the studies fail to find an effect, and those that do are either fatally flawed on methodological grounds or cannot be repro-duced. Other reviewers of this literature have reached the same conclusion." (my underlining)

The authors, first-rate social psychologists at the University of California at Santa Cruz, are specifically critical of Dr. Key's claims:

> "And what of Key's evidence for the effective-ness of subliminal seduction? Most of the studies he reports lack a control or comparison group. Finding

that 62% of all subjects feel sexual, romantic, or satisfied when they see a gin ad with the word sex
embedded in the ice cubes tells us nothing of the
effectiveness of the sex implant. What would hap-
pen if the word sex was removed from the cubes?
Perhaps 62% of the subjects would still feel sexy,
romantic, or satisfied. Perhaps more, perhaps less
would feel this way. Without such a comparison, we
just do not know."

Dr. Key is quick to admit he has no "clear, specific proof that
subliminals affect behavior." When asked for proof during his university lectures, Dr. Key readily confesses he has none!

"Nor do I know anyone else who has clear, specific, simplistic (sic) demonstrable data to settle the
question once and for all."

I suspect Dr. Key hasn't taken the time to look very hard. There
has been a torrent of research on the subject published in an array
of journals: Journal of Marketing, Journal of Advertising, Journal
of Advertising Research, etc., etc. An entire special issue of
Psychology & Marketing was devoted to the subject in the Winter
of 1988. Other work was reported in the Journal of Abnormal
Psychology, the Journal of Experimental Psychology, Cognitive
Psychology, Perception and Psychophysics, the Journal of
Abnormal and Social Psychology, the Journal of Verbal Learning
and Verbal Behavior, the Canadian Journal of Psychology, the
Psychological Review, etc., etc.

The scientific research indicating subliminal advertising does-
n't work is simply overwhelming.

Stephen McDaniel, Sandra Hart, and James McNeal compiled
an excellent review of the literature of subliminal stimulation for a
1982 issue of the Mid-Atlantic Journal of Business.

The research team acknowledged that some early studies —
most now nullified — suggest subliminal messages may have contributed to heightening of one's basic physiological drives (i.e.
hunger, thirst, sex, etc.).

But their review of studies suggesting possible effects on

behavior itself strongly indicates "the ineffectiveness of subliminal advertising."

> "Particularly significant," the team concludes, "is the technique's unproven ability to alter consumer buying behavior. Consumers seem to have psychological 'screening mechanisms' that shield against influences aimed at changing their behavior."

Joel Saegert, brilliant researcher from the University of Texas at San Antonio, writes in a 1979 Journal of Advertising Research:

> "...there simply isn't <u>any</u> published literature that demonstrates the effectiveness of subliminal stimuli in a marketing application."

He added in the same study that dozens of subliminal experiments had not made their way into the research journals because they had not supported the null hypothesis. That is, no market behavior changes resulted from the use of subliminals, therefore the researcher didn't bother to publish his or her findings.

Saegert addressed the issue again in 1987. He discounted any studies indicating subliminal effectiveness in a carefully written essay in Psychology & Marketing: "Why Marketing Should Quit Giving Subliminal Advertising the Benefit of the Doubt."

Sid Dudley, an Associate Professor of Marketing at East Carolina University, conducted a thorough review of the literature of the subject the same year for the Akron Business & Economic Review. Dudley reached two conclusions. First, that some communication can occur "without conscious awareness." Subliminals can encourage behavior toward which individuals may already be disposed. "Consequently," he writes, "self-help messages —don't smoke, lose weight, etc. — may work by providing encouragement to people who are trying to help themselves." To put it another way, if you're willing to part with $15 or more for a tape on which you hear nothing but ocean waves, you have already demonstrated a willingness to help yourself — whether or not the message "under the waves" ever gets through to your subconscious or not.

Dudley's second conclusion is more to the point:

"The possibility that subliminal stimulation offers an effective means of controlling consumer or political behavior is highly unlikely. Claims that it does so seem to be based on enthusiasm rather than hard evidence. Such claims are not supported by published evidence. The available evidence suggests that subliminal messages have little or no persuasive power."

Two fairly recent studies found subliminal effects in a product demonstration environment.

The first of these used 48 Canadian undergraduates, divided into three groups. All subjects watched a two minute "training film" on the proper way to wash fine woolen garments. The demonstrator in the film used a plain white package of soap.

However, a subliminal picture of the Woolite product package was flashed during the film to a group of 18. A subliminal picture of a soap product called Zero was flashed to a group of 16. And the control group of 14 received no subliminal flashes or messages of any kind.

The only difference in the three conditions was the presence or absence of the subliminal "communication." Subjects were then shown pictures of five soap product packages, including Woolite and Zero. The students ranked Zero higher than the other four brands, at statistically significant levels. And the authors conclude that "subliminal stimulation can have an impact on stated preference."

At the same time, the authors freely admit that Zero is "a woolen cleaning product well known in Maritime Canada and widely available." While Woolite was "not widely available at the time and advertised only on cable and not the local network television stations."

The second study was headed by William Kilbourne, on the faculty at Sam Houston State University. Kilbourne et al used a matched set of magazine advertisements: one set with embeds, another set without. Advertised products were Chivas Regal Scotch and Marlboro cigarettes. Subjects registered greater believability in the Chivas Regal advertisements containing embeds, than those without. Results were mixed as far as the Marlboro ads were concerned.

Again Saegert finds serious methodological faults with both studies. His scrutiny of each study is exhaustive. His conclusion in a lengthy Psychology & Marketing article in 1987, is "that spokespersons for the marketing and advertising disciplines can dismiss subliminal advertising from further consideration as a potential promotional technique, at least more conclusively than they have done so in the past."

Later in the same review he declares:

"...procedures for the development of commercial exploitation appear so unlikely that subliminal advertising can be said not to constitute a viable mass communications approach.

The lay public will no doubt continue to be intrigued by the possibility of subliminal advertising, but this should not make us, as marketing theorists and practitioners any more willing to consider an idea with so little to recommend it."

An excellent earlier study by Steven Kelly, a marketing professor at DePaul university, and a consultant to Chicago area advertising agencies, researched the possibility that subliminals might have a positive effect on brand and illustration recall. His research appeared in a 1979 Journal of Advertising. Its title: "Subliminal Embeds in Print Advertising: A Challenge to Advertising Ethics."

An interesting part of Kelly's research was his use of copies of seven original advertisements from one or the other of Dr. Key's first two books for a "treatment group" dummy magazine. Dr. Key claimed that each of the seven ads contained a flurry of subliminal embeds. The "control group" publication contained seven advertisements, very similar to the others in their creative treatment of the product and other elements, but with no discernible embeds.

His findings? Subliminal embeds (if, indeed, there were any in Dr. Key's original selected group) do not generate significant recall of either a brand or its illustration. Either immediately, or after an elapsed time.

Perhaps the most comprehensive study negating possible sub-liminal effects was that conducted under the guidance of the great-ly respected Dr. Myron Gable at Shippenburg University. Before joining the academic world Dr. Gable spent 25 years in industry. A former President of the American Collegiate Retailing Association, Dr. Gable headed the research team of educators in management and marketing. The experiments were reported in a 1987 Journal of Advertising.

The authors contend:

> "This experiment is different from other studies in that product items were photographed with two sets of photographs produced. Deliberate embed-ding was undertaken on one of the two sets of pho-tographs. Four product classifications — camera, pen, beer, and food — were used to test the research question of the effect of embedded sexual stimuli in graphics. These items were selected because all are familiar to, and being purchased by the subjects."

In order to isolate the experimental variable, photographs were used, rather than advertisements. One photograph for each product was embedded by a professional commercial artist. More than 400 subjects were involved in the preference sampling of each product. The authors conducted statistical analyses for each of the product categories across the entire sample, and by gender.

They found no differences in preference between males and females for embedded vs. non-embedded illustrations.

In two instances (beer and food) the non-embedded illustration was preferred by the total sample; in the case of the camera illus-tration, no clear-cut preference could be found. And in the case of the pen, the embed illustration was preferred.

The authors felt that since non-embedded illustrations were chosen in two categories, and no significant preference was shown for another category, the one "indication of preference was simply not great enough to say that it could be anything but a chance occurrence."

Their conclusion:

"The researchers have been able to empirically establish that subliminally embedded sexual words and/or symbols in product photographs do not significantly influence college-age consumer preference toward embedded product illustrations. There were no significant preference differences between the photos of products that had embeds in them and those that did not.

This controlled test rejects Key's notion that titillating words and/or symbols embedded within advertisements can manipulate consumer preference. Moreover, the results of this experiment indicate no differences when the data were analyzed by gender.

Haberstroh's research has called Key's charges 'preposterous, absurd, ludicrous, laughable.' He bases his conclusions on interviews with ad people associated with half a dozen of Key's advertising examples and a random survey of art directors of 100 advertising agencies. Moore concluded his review of the literature by stating '...subliminal directives have not been shown to have the power ascribed to them by advocates of subliminal advertising.' The present research provides strong empirical reinforcement to the aforementioned positions because it is based on the results of a controlled experiment wherein the only factor that could influence personal preferences of respondents was the embedded material."

The research team agrees that there simply is no reason for advertisers and their agencies to embed sexually loaded words, symbols, or organs in print advertising.

In short, they don't work.

John Vokey and Don Read of the University of Lethbridge in Alberta, Canada, reached the same conclusion. In their skillfully written and carefully researched article for the November 1985 issue of the American Psychologist, they question, again and again, Dr. Key's evidence for many of his claims. When, for instance, Dr.

Key finds that 95% of the college males who were shown an embedded Playboy promotional advertisement displaying a chesty nude female (Fig. 15), recalled it a month later, Vokey and Read suggest that "it is quite possible that college-males would have remembered the ad equally well without the embedded imagery." The research evidence presented by Dr. Key that the subliminal embedding (The "chestnuts" in the wreath are the heads of penises.) is responsible for the high rate of recall is patently vapid.

In another example Dr. Key claims that there's an overwhelming preference by his students for a particular kind of Bacardi rum advertised in Playboy, Time, and Esquire. (Fig. 16) Dr. Key states that the words "u buy" are embedded in the photograph of Ron Anejo, the preferred rum. He could locate no embeds in the other three Bacardi rums also advertised in the same ad. Thus — he reasons — it was the unseen two-word message in the ad that contributed to the strong preference by his undergraduate subjects for Ron Anejo. The Lethbridge University team points out, however, that the preferred Ron Anejo:

> "...is the only one with the words 'extra special'
> clearly announced on the label, is of a much darker
> color than all the others, is the only one presented in
> a high-status brandy snifter, and comes in a larger
> bottle. In contrast, in Key's view, only the presence
> of the subliminal message provides a plausible
> explanation for his subjects' preference." (Fig. 16)

In yet another example they rebut Dr. Key's claim that copywriters and advertising artists subliminally insert the word "sex" and other sexually oriented words into their advertisements in order to enhance memorability.

Vokey and Read produced sets of slides made from vacation photographs. On one set the word "sex" was embedded three or four times on each slide. A nonsense word (random vowels and consonants) was embedded in the same location as the word "sex," on each slide of another set. Nothing was embedded on a third set.

The three slide sets were then shown to nearly 100 subjects. One half saw them immediately, the other half two days later. The team's finding:

"Despite Key's claims and concerns, slides that had been sex-embedded during initial exposure were no better recognized than slides in either of the two control conditions. Nor did retention of the originally sex-embedded slides improve as a function of the retention interval."

In short, a "sex" embed won't help you to remember the ad!

Embedding the words "HERSHEY'S CHOCOLATE" didn't help the sale of Hershey's products either. At least that's what Stephen George of Mulunani Research in Hawaii and Luther Jennings of Occidental College discovered in a highly controlled purchase-situation research study in 1975.

The fascinating report was published in a 1975 issue of Perceptual and Motor Skills. Subjects watched a movie in which the words "HERSHEY'S CHOCOLATE" (one word above the other, each word 2 1/2 inches high) were superimposed on the screen below the detection threshold. Subjects, all college undergraduates, were divided into two groups. A control group watched the movie containing no subliminal words. An experimental group watched the same movie, but with the undetectable words "HERSHEY'S CHOCOLATE" flashed twenty times during the film.

The only source of candy bars within a four-mile radius of the site of the experiment was the college student store. Subjects had no public or private means of transportation to any other location selling candy. At the college student store the following candy was available: Hershey's Chocolate Bars, Hershey's Almond Bars, Hershey's Kisses, Nestle's Milk Chocolate Bars, Nestle's Almond Bars, and Nestle's Crunch Bars, in both 5¢ and 10¢ sizes.

The sale of chocolate candy at the student store was carefully monitored — under a clever ruse. Students buying any of the brands above were required to fill out a bogus survey for a local radio station. The results?

During the ten days of the experiment no student in either the experimental or control group purchased <u>any</u> Hershey's product in the student store.

Their conclusion:

"Obviously, the results do not support the con-
tentions of motivational research theorists. Neither
experimental nor control students purchased any
Hershey's product, let alone Hershey's Chocolate
Bars." (underlining mine)

Dr. Timothy Moore, a highly respected researcher in psychology and education at York University in Toronto, pooh-poohs possible effects subliminal messages might have on market behavior.

He reviews much of the literature on the subject in a lengthy
article in the Spring, 1982 issue of the Journal of Marketing.
Analyzing and critiquing the work of Harris et al (1979), Wright
(1973), Zuckerman (1960), McConnell et al (1958), and Anastasi
(1964) he asks in the title of the article: "Could subliminally presented stimuli have a marketing application?"

"Subliminal stimuli are usually so weak that the
recipient is not just unaware of the stimulus but is
also oblivious to the fact that he/she is being stimulated. As a result, the potential effects of subliminal
stimuli are easily nullified by other ongoing stimulation in the same sensory channel or by attention
being focused on another modality. These factors
pose serious difficulties for any possible marketing
application.

...subliminal directives have not been shown to
have the power ascribed to them by advocates of
subliminal advertising. In general, the literature on
subliminal perception shows that the most clearly
documented effects are obtained only in highly contrived and artificial situations. These effects, when
present, are brief and of small magnitude. The result
is perhaps best construed as an epiphenomenon — a
subtle and fleeting by-product of the complexities of
human cognitive activity. These processes have no
apparent relevance to the goals of advertising.

...the fine print near the bottom of an ad is likely to be far more important than any concealed genitalia could be."

In a 1988 Psychology & Marketing essay, Dr. Moore again reviews the literature of subliminals and adds an exclamation point to his 1982 findings:

> "...advertisers have nothing to gain from using subliminal techniques."

One ballyhooed study suggesting a degree of effectiveness in stirring in some subliminals into advertising was a 1983 experiment conducted by a team of researchers at NeuroCommunications Research Laboratories in Danbury, Connecticut. Sidney Weinstein, President of the firm, his son Curt, and Ronald Drozdenko, found that subliminals could enhance purchase behavior.

Basically, Weinstein and his group found an "inclination to purchase" candy advertised on paper "watermarked" with the subliminal word "buy." Participants, however, who viewed a book advertisement "watermarked" with the word "sex" showed no such purchase inclination.

In January, 1984 Weinstein offered readers of Ad Age topline reports of his unusual finding, and was inundated by requests. Many were from reporters and TV program producers who were alarmed over the use of "immoral" subliminal procedures.

Weinstein, however, later admitted the alleged purchase inclination effect for the candy may have been caused by differences in the appearance of the papers (reflection, background complexity, etc.) on which the respective ads were printed. He made the startling announcement in a paper he delivered at the June, 1984 Advertising and Consumer Psychology Conference in New York. The conference was co-sponsored by Ted Bates Advertising, the Marketing Science Institute, and the American Psychological Association. Papers given there were printed in a volume titled: *Advertising and Consumer Psychology* in 1986.

Curt Weinstein, now President of NeuroCommunications, revealed some doubts about the original study when I spoke with him in June, 1992. He remembers subjects holding the "buy" advertisements up to the light, and remarking "I see something...there's some printing on this sheet, etc." He admits the message may not have been subliminal.

"It's not the way to advertise. Why not just come right out and say 'buy my book?'" he further stated. "Don't bury the message. It's hard enough to get people to buy a book with supraliminal language. I don't think subliminal advertising has any effect," he added.

Pratkanis and Greenwald summarize their attitude toward the effectiveness of subliminals in the marketplace with this comment from their Psychology & Marketing Research article in 1988:

> "This review does little to change the recommendation of Moore (1982), Ogilvy (1983), Saegert (1987), and various textbook writers: Aaker and Myers, 1987; Engele, Blackwell, and Miniard, 1986; Mowen, 1987, that subliminal procedures offer little or nothing of value to the marketplace practitioner. There continues to be no reliable evidence in support of the more sensational claims for the power of subliminal influence.
>
> Our review suggests that those concerned with marketing ethics would have more societal impact if they discussed such questions as, 'Under what conditions are the use of such tactics legitimate?' and 'What can be done about the unethical abuse of nonconscious process?' as opposed to continually worrying about the sensational, but apparently nonexistent, processes of subliminal persuasion and seduction."

Other textbook writers agree. Bovee and Arens, authors of the world's largest selling advertising text, Contemporary Advertising, conclude that no messages are being received through subliminal techniques.

And, like other researchers, wonder why no practitioner — or ex-practitioner — comes forward and admits to using this technique:

> "As far as Mr. Key's idea of the insidious cunning of marketing decision makers goes, it is interesting to note that in more than 600 pages on the subject, he mentions not a single individual who

admits to, or even accuses others of, being involved in subliminal embedding."

Wells, Burnett, and Moriarty reason in *Advertising, Principles and Practice*, that the real issue is whether or not subliminals can affect <u>buying behavior</u>, and conclude:

> "These (subliminal) processes have no apparent relevance to the goals of advertising."

Dunn, Barban, Krugman, and Reid find that:

> "Although public awareness of subliminal techniques has increased over the past two decades, scientific support for the practical effectiveness of subliminal advertising is limited and contradictory."

Patti and Frazer cite a number of reasons to discount Dr. Key's "psychusations." I enjoyed this particular very "practical" reason:

> "...it is incredible that many readers could be expected to receive the subliminal messages, which seem to require a great deal of imagination to perceive, even when one's attention is directed to them. Even the simpler goal of merely getting consumers to notice a brand name is a very difficult job for most advertisers, since consumers have a highly developed ability to ignore advertising. The notion that they could perceive hidden elements in ads while failing to notice the most prominent elements seems most unlikely."

Roy Paul Nelson, in his popular *The Design of Advertising*, makes some allowance for the handful of kooks embedding kinky messages in their artwork:

> "No doubt a few sophomoric people in the creative end of advertising do sneak double meanings into the art and copy of some advertising in order to play the clown; but to argue that there is a conspiracy in advertising to actually sell products through subliminal devices is probably unwarranted."

Many other advertising textbook authors, however, have chosen to ignore the subject. One must assume they consider the idea so ludicrous they don't think it worthy of discussion in their texts. A few such authors are: Jewler, Runyon, Mandel, Bolen, and Engel.

A study carried out in 1970 by Del Hawkins of the University of Oregon has been cited ad nauseam as "living proof" that sub-liminally embedded messages do indeed affect basic drives. In this instance, thirst. The Hawkins study concluded that a subliminal message can "directly affect consumption-relevant behavior." Indeed, groups exposed to the subliminal stimulus "Drink Coke" and the supraliminal stimulus "Coke," were thirstier after the experiment than a similar group exposed to nonsense syllables in the same way as the experimental group.

However, a later study, which he carried out with Sharon Beatty of the University of Alabama, was far more extensive and was pub-lished in a 1989 Journal of Advertising. Hawkins and Beatty dis-covered that his 1970 experiment had a sampling error. That the control group (which watched subliminal and supraliminal non-sense syllables) reporting lower thirst ratings was simply due to chance. Their conclusion:

> "...this study (the 1989 study) casts serious doubts on the validity of one of the few studies to provide empirical evidence of subliminal effects in an advertising context."

(They were, of course, alluding to Hawkins' 1970 research)

From available research on the effectiveness of subliminal advertising in the marketplace, the conclusion is inescapable that it has none — either in a positive or negative direction. Buying behavior, ad memorability, and other communication drive indices remain unchanged, or show insignificant movement when sublimi-nals are added to advertising.

Because subliminal advertising's practical applicability to mar-ket behavior is so flimsy, one is tempted to question the power of the subconscious to alter behavior. Or, at the very least, to question the efficacy of subliminal messages in modifying behavior of any kind.

Though outside the rather narrow purview of this small volume, the alleged power of self-improvement subliminal tapes invariably arises in classroom conversations dealing with subliminal advertising. Do they work, or don't they?

These tapes allegedly can modify behavior — from curbing TV snacking to conquering impotence. Others claim to unleash musical ability, dispel anger, and produce wild and colorful dreams. Still others are intended for your children: "A Messy Child's Guide to Neatness," "Developing Good Study Habits," and "Potty Training for Toddlers."

For a time in the 70s, it seemed de rigueur for psychology students working on Master's degrees to devise simplistic subliminal behavior modification tests,using children and fellow graduate students as guinea pigs. Invariably there was no change in reading scores, math scores, or any kind of score as the result of listening to subaudible self-improvement tapes. Or "seeing" invisible subliminal messages splashed on screens.

My advice? Save your money.

In study after study — Severance and Dyer, Hovsepian and Quatman, George and Jennings — psychological and communications researchers have found little or no influence on behavior from using subliminals.

One tape sold by Psychodynamics in Zephyr Cove (!), Nevada, is labeled "Sex Attraction/Sex Appeal." The brochure's promotional copy about the tape reads:

> "Become an aphrodisiac to the opposite sex. Awaken natural attraction instincts. Turn on unique sex appeal. Increase sexual encounters. Use with caution, discretion, and a fast pair of sneakers!"

For $14.95 I received a cassette containing pleasant elevator music on one side, and the sound of ocean waves on the other. Perhaps I don't play it often enough...but after three years of listening to it I'm still waiting for the need to use a fast pair of sneakers.

Some of the cloying embedded copy, too faint to hear, reads

like sophomoric blather:

> "I can enjoy my sexual maturity. Love comes
> easily to me. Honesty, sincerity, kindness and
> integrity are also forms of love. I am honest and sin-
> cere with my love. Etc., etc., etc."

Other tapes promise "success, fulfillment, and unlimited happi-
ness." Just send in your order, and $14.95 for most tapes, no mat-
ter which tape hustler you're dealing with. Yep, $14.95 plus a cou-
ple dollars for postage and handling...and voila! More sex than you
can handle, a winning self-image, and the six winning numbers in
next Saturday's Lotto. Be able to read like lightning, remember
more than elephants have forgotten, and never grow old.
Yep...imagine all that subliminal swamp land...for only $14.95.
Unbelievable!

Brooklyn College psychology professor, Arthur Reber, calls the
tapes "worthless trash." Kevin Krajick, writing for Newsweek in
1990, claims that:

> "Most psychologists, while acknowledging that
> experiments show people can sometimes process
> sounds or sights so slight they can't be consciously
> perceived, say there's no evidence such stimuli
> change lives."

Eric Eich, a professor of psychology at the University of British
Columbia, puts it this way in the same article:

> "Any time you get off your butt to improve
> yourself, you'll probably see results...if you've just
> spent money on a tape, you'll claim it helped."

Tape firms are selling more than $50 million of self-help sub-
liminal tapes a year. One of the largest companies, producing
between 50,00 and 60,000 tapes a month, is Potentials Unlimited in
Grand Rapids, Michigan.

Its president is "hypnotherapist" Barrie Konicov, 53.
Newsweek pointed out that his scientific credentials consist of
stints at selling aluminum hair curlers, fire alarms, and life insurance. That is, until his life insurance selling license was jerked in

1972 for forgery. A federal judge once described Konicov's hyp-
notherapeutic qualifications as a degree in marketing and approximately "three weekend seminars on hypnosis."

Potentials Unlimited was ordered in 1984 to erase all copies of
31 different self-help cassettes which claimed to promise relief
from maladies as diverse as warts to high blood pressure. However,
many of the same tapes are still being happily promoted — with
slightly altered titles.

Another tape producer, Paul Tuthill, president of Michigan-
based Mind Communications, claimed that playing phrases such as
"I do it today" and "I take action now" under a "bed" of classical
music, encouraged more office productivity. "The good people (in
Tuthill's office) improved immensely, and the people who were
marginal or shirkers quit."

Again, his observation lacked a control group for purposes of
comparison. And we are left with little verification for the tape's
effectiveness other than the tape manufacturer's hyperbole.

Etc. etc. etc., an American Society of Advertising and
Promotion newsletter, reports the comments of two authorities on
alleged results from using behavior modification tapes.

> "Susan Brayfield-Cave, a clinical psychologist,
> reports that subliminal messages affect different
> people in different ways. In order for any kind of
> therapy to help, it must be tailored to your personal
> moods. A mass-produced tape couldn't guarantee
> the same results for everyone."

Interesting point. Advertising brochures for subliminal-mes-
sage self-help tapes invariably claim similar success for all who
buy them.

Psychiatrist Dr. Robert Weiss goes even further.

> "The tapes are no more effective than reading a
> book or having a conversation. It's not technically
> possible for something to do anything for you with-
> out your own cooperation. And how do we know
> exactly what kind of information you will be recep-

tive to at a certain time?"

Howard Shevrin, a professor of psychology at the University of Michigan, is one of the most outspoken critics of self-help tapes in the country. He's been researching subliminal effects for more than 30 years.

Writing in the Middletown, New York Daily Times-Herald, Evelyn Nieves asked Professor Shevrin for his opinions about self-improvement tapes. His response:

> "They're snake oil. They can't deliver what they advertise and claim. It's all anecdotal evidence, the bottom line is that they cannot cite any scientific research to substantiate their claims. The way they confuse people is that there's a good deal of research evidence, including my own, that subliminal messages do register. But that's a far cry from concluding that because a message registers, it will have the desired effect and change behavior. They're two separate claims."

A major subliminal tape entrepreneur was "black box" inventor, Dr. Hal Becker. The founder of tiny Behavioral Engineering Center in Metairie, Louisiana, Dr. Becker would like to see subliminals flashing away at us during programs on television. Messages, for instance, aimed at the chronically fat, bad drivers, or drug users. He told a Time Magazine writer in 1979 that with subliminal tapes airing constantly on TV:

> "We could eliminate weight problems in one generation, reduce auto insurance by 50%."

Rather than hype his behavior modifying tapes to the public, he claims he sold or leased them to department stores, real estate firms, retail outlets, and psychologists.

Dr. Becker maintains that some 50 department stores in the United States and Canada were using his "black boxes" back in 1978. Dr. Becker's "black box" was issued a U.S. patent in October of 1966. It sells for close to $10,000, or it could be leased for $5,000 a year.

These instruments mix laid-back mood music with undetectable anti-shoplifting messages, supposedly whispered 9,000 times an hour. The message? "Be honest. Do not steal. I am honest. I will not steal. But...if I do steal, I will be caught and sent to jail."

Dr. Becker has repeatedly claimed that one East Coast department store chain reduced shoplifting 37% in a nine-month trial. But when I asked Dr. Becker for the name of the chain a few years ago, he refused to identify the stores. He also adamantly refused to give me the name of any of the fifty stores in which he supposedly had "black box" installations. Adding to the riddle is the unwillingness of any business firm to admit it has used Dr. Becker's device.

We are left with unsubstantiated and suspicious shoplifting reduction claims by the inventor and chief salesman for the very device allegedly responsible for reductions in store theft. Dr. Becker admitted in 1985 that he was no longer involved with his "black box" creation. But he did say he was a consultant for another similar operation, Proactive Systems, Inc. in Portland, Oregon.

Proactive Systems' anti-theft messages are often aired without a "carrier" (e.g. music, ocean waves, etc.) in retail establishments. Retailers can request one of several different messages on a micro computer chip: "I am an honest person." "I do not steal." "Stay honest. Do not steal." or "I respect private property." These messages are most often played just below the audible level of store noise, getting louder — but still inaudible — as store traffic increases.

In 1985, David Tyler, at that time President of Proactive, told me that the J. Jacobs Department Stores, headquartered in Seattle, were using his subliminal messaging system. Officials of the 300-store chain, however, refused to confirm the system was being used.

Recently, however, John Richardson, Director of Loss Prevention at the chain since 1980, told me that the company had used the system for a year in 20 of their 300 stores. He said the firm conducted the test during 1984-1985. "I'm not sold on it," he said. "Statistically, some of the stores improved slightly, but others showed actual increases in shrinkage," he claimed.

During the test the following message was undetectable under soft "elevator" music:

"Stay Honest. Don't Steal."

Proactive Systems, Inc. went out of business shortly after the 1984-1985 J. Jacobs Department Stores experiment.

Detecting a nationwide need for improvement in the bedroom — and on the golf course — Stimutech, Inc. of East Lansing, Michigan began marketing a line of microchip self-improvement messages in 1983. Stimutech's Expando-Vision offered eight individual self-help programs which could be interfaced with one's personal computer and played over the television set.

One-inch high messages are flashed on the TV screen for 1/30th of a second, at 60-second intervals during normal programming. Hardly subliminal, messages such as "I will eat less!" march quickly across one's TV screen.

Of course subliminal messages are also said to be embedded in movies and music. The "Exorcist" was accused of containing undetectable embeds. Warner Brothers, producers of the film, indeed, admitted that there were at least two embedded "subliminal" frames, death mask flashes at 1/48th of a second, inserted into the film. Their effect, if any, would be pure speculation.

Another movie producer admitted he was using a subliminal filming technique in the making of "My World Dies Screaming." The word "Blood" was subliminally flashed on the screen, supposedly to heighten emotion. Whether it did or not is anyone's guess..

A television station in Wichita, Kansas, tried to convince an at-large murderer to give himself up by flashing subliminal messages on the TV screen. Of course, without success.

Subliminal messages have also been said to appear on the covers of Beatles record albums. And subaudible messages were allegedly inserted into "Strawberry Fields" and other songs. Supposedly, other rock songs have also been similarly infected. What effect? Who knows.

The parents of two young men who made a suicide pact after listening to allegedly embedded Judas Priest music, sued the heavy-metal band and CBS records. Raymond Belknap, 18, and James Vance, 20, both from Sparks, Nevada, blew away their brains with a shotgun after an afternoon of pot smoking, beer drinking, and listening to the "Stained Class" Judas Priest album.

Judge Jerry Carr Whitehead, however, found in favor of the Judas Priest band and its record company, CBS Records, declaring:

> "The scientific research presented does not establish that subliminal stimuli, even if perceived, may precipitate conduct of this magnitude. There exist other factors which explain the conduct of the deceased independent of the subliminal stimuli."

The most exhaustive research on the impact of embedded messages in rock music was performed by a Canadian research team at the University of Lethbridge in Alberta in 1984. John Vokey and Don Read explored the phenomenon of "backmasking." This is nothing more than inserting an undetected message into a record by playing the message backwards. The words cannot be consciously perceived when the record is played in its normal, forward manner. In addition to Dr. Key, a small gaggle of vociferous preachers has proclaimed that these imperceptible communications are heard at the unconscious level, and may have been placed in the records by Satan himself!

The intent of the messages is invariably evil. The ministers declare that the backmasked messages have had a devastating effect on society. They claim that individuals who listen to rock music, and the backmasking, are more likely to become drunks, druggies, criminals, and sexual miscreants. Which, of course, overlooks widely recognized evidence that age is the principal discriminator in such anti-social behavior — as well as the most significant indicator of rock music enjoyment.

The Lethridge team tested the hypothesis that backmasked messages are "manifested in an unconscious manner on the listeners' subsequent behavior." Many conservative sermonizers, of course, feel that the rock and rap generation is being led to booze, drugs, and illicit sex without being aware of it. Through unheard backmasked messages in rock music. To test that theory, the Canadian professors devised a very creative research design.

Of course they couldn't use the promotion of drugs, etc. in their research. They decided to use something less illegal: spelling.

Would backmasked spelling cues help in a significant fashion the correct spelling of homophones (words that have different meanings, but sound the same, like "feet" and "feat")? They backmasked a series of sentences, each of which gave an individual homophone its meaning. Example: "Climbing a mountain is a remarkable 'feat.'" The researchers thought:

> "...if the subjects are comprehending the backward messages unconsciously, their spelling of the biased homophones should reflect that comprehension."

However, there was no effect — either positive or negative — on subjects' spelling due to the backmasked explanatory sentences.

"Taken together with the results of the other tasks," they concluded, "we could find no evidence that our listeners were influenced, consciously or unconsciously, by the content of backward messages."

Heber Sharp of Utah State University in a much earlier, but somewhat similar study, found that subliminal embeds actually improved student test scores. His research appeared in a 1959 Journal of Applied Psychology. He revealed, however, that 60% of his test subjects had learned consciously to detect the presence of the "subliminals," thus invalidating his experiment.

Finally, Dr. Lloyd Silverman, a research psychologist at the Veterans Administration Regional Office in New York City, has claimed startling positive therapeutic results in using subliminals on schizophrenics and manic depressives. He shows these psychotics and neurotics such messages as "Mommy and I Are One," "Fuck Mommy," and "Beating Dad is OK," at speeds too fast to read. His studies have convinced him, at least, that these subliminal blinks can alter the behavior positively of his subjects — for a short time at least.

But his colleagues in psychology aren't convinced. When Virginia Adams wrote an article about his work in a 1982 issue of Psychology Today, more than a dozen psychologists to whom she talked, refused to endorse his findings.

Saegert also found serious methodological flaws in Silverman's

1976 study as well as a 1986 counterpart by Silverman and Weinberger.

Chapter 5

OK, so <u>why</u> <u>bother</u> with it?

Chapter 5

OK, so <u>why</u> <u>bother</u> with it?

If you're wondering why in the world you're reading a book about something you can't see, hear, feel, or even smell, I can understand. Many in the world of advertising agree with you. They are hoping that Dr. Wilson Bryan Key and all the hokey-pokey he finds in ice cube artwork will just go away. Let's hold our breath, they think. And don't write or say a word about him.

Surely he'll disappear. And take his Parkay patties, gin tonics, clam plates, cake mixes, Calvert cocktails, Horsman dolls, and Ritz crackers with him.

Sorry. Not only has he not disappeared, his theories may be more popular than ever.

Subliminal advertising reappeared as top-of-the-line cocktail party conversation in 1973 with the publication of Dr. Key's *Subliminal Seduction*. And the advertising world's been eating his dust ever since. Surely, we thought, the nutty notion that ice cubes spell "S-E-X" would pass quickly.

But, three years later he shoved sexy Ritz crackers down our throats with *Media Sexploitation*. In 1980 it was bestiality-on-a-placemat with *Clam-Plate Orgy*. And the truly outrageous fellatio-with-the-Pope in his 1989 *The Age of Manipulation*.

He has accused the entire advertising industry of a monstrous conspiracy to sell products using blatantly deceitful techniques. Techniques it had never occurred to most advertising practitioners to use!

His accusations are serious, and most Americans believe him! He lambastes the advertising community, and all of its practition-ers, for intentionally inserting invisible words and organs into the advertising it creates.

He then links this miasma to a happily colluding mass media in a giant plot to "mindlessly pursue (our) self-destruction."

Even advertising educators do not escape his acerbic comments. They have "unpardoningly failed" to alert students to what's really going on in the mass media.

U.S. society, he maintains, is now being deliberately subverted, disoriented, and "very possibly destroyed" by embeds in media advertising! They are "an integral part of modern American life — even though they have never been seen by many people at the conscious level."

Serious charges, indeed.

While young, well educated Americans have accepted his theories without question, how has the professional advertising community — those tens of thousands of practitioners — responded to his attack on their dicey craft?

Let me put it this way. A gnat on a hippo's hiney will get more reaction from the hippo than my professional advertising colleagues are giving Dr. Key's finger-pointing. All know it's just so much naughty nonsense.

Ignore it, they say. And like the tumescent nipples he sees in your over-rocks martini, they'll go away when the ice melts.

A few advertising practitioners are outraged, of course. But even fewer make a fuss about it. Let's all keep calm, they suggest, and let the provocative professor run out of gas. For god's sake let's not give him any more publicity. Let's just pretend he doesn't exist. He'll go away.

The problem? He and his notions aren't going away.

On the contrary.

The let's-all-hunker-down-and-burrow-our-collective-heads-ever-deeper-under-Madison-Avenue hasn't worked! Advertising agencies, buyers of more research than any other institution in the world, should have recognized the trend-line years ago! And, instead of remaining mute, screamed "fraud!"

On September 17, 1984 Advertising Age published a 4,000-word cover piece in which I scolded the advertising industry for its silence on subliminal advertising. "Advertising practitioners," I wrote, "ignore Dr. Wilson Bryan Key and his accusations at their own risk. Often that ignorance can be embarrassing. Thousands of students are graduating every year thoroughly conversant with Dr. Key, his books, and theories. Many may have heard or seen him personally. And some are quick to believe the worst about advertising and its practitioners."

No one, ad executives will tell you, believes any of his claptrap. Let's all just clam up, and let him rust in peace.

That strategy simply hasn't worked. And how long will it take the ad industry to realize it hasn't worked? Dr. Key has achieved a permanent place in American advertising folklore. "Like him, loathe him, he's here to stay." I wrote those words in Ad Age ten years ago. They are as true today as they were then!

I begged my professional advertising colleagues to give his "feverish fantasies" a thorough airing. "While many advertising professionals sit mutely," I warned, "and advertising publications report nothing about the issue, Dr. Key is in the hustings, making converts by the thousands. It is," I wrote, "an issue about which we must no longer remain mute."

That position received solid support from academe — nine years later! In their excellent study of the public's perception of subliminal advertising in a 1993 Journal of Advertising Research, professors Rogers and Smith concluded that:

> ...marketers must be concerned about public attitudes toward subliminal advertising. It is not enough for advertising professionals to agree among themselves that subliminal advertising doesn't work and therefore isn't used. Even if consumers' beliefs about subliminal advertising are inaccurate, it is nevertheless these beliefs that help shape consumer reactions toward ads and attitudes about the advertising industry.

Fred Danzig, Ad Age editor at the time, told me several weeks later, that the article generated the greatest outpouring of letters-to-the-editor in the history of that publication. What surprised me, however, was the tone — and content — of many of the letters.

Most were very defensive, if not insulting.

Jock Elliott, Jr., former Chairman of the Board of Ogilvy & Mather, put much of the blame for the spread of Dr. Key's titillating trash on us college professors, and our institutions of higher learning:

> "Gosh, Jack Haberstroh's article on 'subliminal advertising' (AA, Sept. 17) makes me mad. What he says, in effect, is that Wilson Bryan Key is a quack but that a lot of people, including students, believe his quackery, and that 'advertising practitioners ignore him at their own risk.' Well and good. Except that we don't ignore him. Every time we practitioners visit a campus (which is pretty often), we are almost invariably asked about subliminal advertising. Our continual explanations that the practice simply doesn't exist are usually met with varying degrees of skepticism. Why? because Mr. Key has been preaching his hokum _with the blessings of the educational institutions_. I've even run into professors who teach how subliminal advertising works! Prof. Haberstroh reports with seeming alarm that '50% of (his) students to whom Key lectured thought that at least half of all artists willfully were inserting subliminals' and 'some are quick to believe the worst about advertising practitioners.'
>
> Why in heaven's name, did Prof. Haberstroh invite Mr. Key to lecture to his students in the first place? A terrible disservice to advertising and, more important, to his students.
>
> The solution to the perpetuation of this myth is not for the advertising world to speak out but for the academic world to shut up. Prof. Haberstroh writes, 'I discuss his theories every semester in my large advertising classes.' Why, one wonders.
>
> In fact, I wonder why he wrote the article for Ad

Age. If he believes that Mr. Key's theories are 'preposterous, absurd, ludicrous, laughable,' as he says, he could better spend his time saying so to his fellow professors — instead of discussing Mr. Key with his students and providing him with a platform.

A sorry commentary on academe."

Perhaps someone should explain to Mr. Elliott that the primary purpose for going to a university is to learn something. To listen to, and learn from, those who may hold unpopular views. Those who — gasp — may disagree with Mr. Elliott's view-of-the-world.

To host a speaker on a college or university campus in no way, of course, means a campus endorsement of his or her views. But I suspect Mr. Elliott knows that.

No, Key's books and philosophy are popular with tens of millions of Americans, not because a handful of college professors discuss his whackiness with their advertising students. But because the advertising industry sits on its collective hands and remains silent!

No advertising professor I know of (oh, perhaps with one exception) — and remember most profs were at one time practitioners — believes that subliminals are being systematically embedded into advertising. Keep in mind also, that many ad profs continue their professional craft while teaching. We're certainly passing along our views — we're obliged to — on Key's carnal claptrap.

But education, as opposed to indoctrination, demands more than our opinions. Contrary to what Mr. Elliott thinks, it's possible that the college advertising classroom may be the only place where Dr. Key's theories are rigorously discussed. Thoroughly criticized. And perhaps ridiculed.

Robert Funkhouser, VP of Advertising and Public Relations at the Carnation Company, in his letter, likened the subject of subliminal advertising to "a turd in a punch bowl. It's not a very big one, but when it pops up now and then we all stand around and say, 'Ho hum, there's that...again.' I agree with Prof. Haberstroh. We should no longer remain mute. The new Advertising Education Foundation has new resources, and it should target subliminal advertising, expose it, and get it the hell out of our children's classrooms."

Nice thought — this last — but to my knowledge no AEF funds have found their way into a subliminal advertising exposé.

Typical of most of the letters was this dandy from Don J. Folger of Fahlgren & Swink in Marion, Ohio:

> "The recent flap created by the regular reappearance of yet another 'sins of subliminal advertising' guru both amuses and distresses me. My distress centers on the silliness of the situation to any advertising professional. Perhaps that's the reason we don't pay more attention to these academia nuts. Most of us are too busy trying to do a good job for our clients to waste time dignifying a hollow charge with an answer.
>
> My amusement stems from the point that these 'Freudian' scholars miss the boat in their perpetually prurient prattle. If subliminals really worked, why would we waste time, space and money on genitalia and sexual symbolism when it would be much more cost-effective to just say "Buy now!"

And this lulu from Charles B. Jones, an advertising management consultant from Chicago:

> "As a guest lecturer at communications or advertising classes of several universities, I have found myself before students who have been assigned W.B. Key's *Subliminal Seduction* as _required_ reading. In addition, conversations with communication students from other universities have confirmed that these are not isolated instances — that the book is commonly employed as course reading.
>
> Discussions with faculty members have led to admissions that the book is used not because of the validity or merit of the content, but simply because of its prurient and controversial nature. One professor openly admitted, 'It helps keep the kids interest-

ed, if nothing else.' Yet, I have found the students accept Mr. Key's views as gospel.

There is every reason to believe that the majority of the copies of Mr. Key's patently spurious books are purchased by students at the behest of 'academics' — the same people who would deride their counterparts in nuclear physics if they were found to be using 'The Wizard of Oz' or 'Tom Swift and His Electric Grandmother' as required reading. And yet, these same pedants wonder why the advertising industry looks upon their graduates with suspicion, if not dismay."

Several academics jumped into the cauldron, including an N.Y.U. Emeritus Professor of Advertising, Darrell B. Lucas:

"Jock Elliott, Jr. bluntly criticized those in the academic world who inspire fear of subliminal advertising (AA, Oct. 4). He is right! Let me make a point.

A generation has passed since an early claim of effective subliminal advertising stirred the industry. Soon the claim was challenged and experimental money was spent to test the theory. Worry about subliminal advertising faded as evidence proved the technique to have little or no practical potential.

Let me go on a bit further. I taught advertising fulltime in New York, the advertising hub, for more than 40 years. I was blessed with exposure to a host of creative writers. Teachers who imply that most of these designers of advertisements are slyly slipping in subliminal devices are irresponsible and badly informed. And if there are a few advertising professionals who play with a subliminal approach, they are wasting their time. Unfortunately, many teachers of economics, sociology and other social sciences have long been critics of both the advertising function and the advertising business. They find it entertaining, especially for students in elective courses, to treat advertising as an economic waste and also as a threat to the best interests of consumers. The cure cannot be 'for the academic world to shut up.' It won't. Instead, current industry efforts to educate the public, including those in academe, are helpful and must go on."

The Chairman of the Department of Economics and Business Administration, Stewart Lee, at Geneva College in Beaver Falls, Pennsylvania, gave my position some support in another Ad Age letter:

"I think the ad community might want to know that there are some professors of consumer science/consumer education who discredit the idea of subliminal advertising. But the topic does come up, and I believe that it is important to show evidence to counteract Key's *Subliminal Seduction*."

Robert T. Reilly, a Professor of communication at the University of Nebraska, wrote:

"Thanks for the article on subliminal advertising. As a former ad exec, now teaching, I can rely on at least two queries a semester from students who have been informed about this phenomenon. Usually the source is another faculty member, perhaps in the department of sociology, but even, sometimes, in our own department.

I'd like to add a couple of arguments to the analysis provided by Mr. Haberstroh.

1. No one has ever shown WHY these subliminal effects are used. Mr. Key obviously knows nothing about advertising or product positioning (that word probably sounds evil to him), and he considers the role of ads to be corruption, not sales.

2. With all the leads available at the highest level of government, you'd think that some of the purported offenders would discuss their crimes with colleagues. I never heard any such confessions in 35 years of association with the profession. Mr. Key

must posit on one vast vow of silence that permeates the nation's agencies.

3. Mr. Key fails to distinguish between what is really subliminal, by definition, and what is obviously seductive, deliberately provocative. Some ads for items like perfume and deodorants are blatantly sexual and there is nothing subliminal about them.

4. Finally, if these subliminal effects are so clever they defy all but the instructed, why would pragmatic folks like advertising agency members take a chance on something that can't be measured?

Perhaps the reason there isn't more outcry against Mr. key's books is that professionals don't take seriously much of what happens on college campuses. They figure a few weeks in an agency will straighten all those off-the-wall notions out. That's probably true for students who become practitioners, but maybe not for those who become consumers."

This tidbit was included. It's from Blaine S. Greenfield, an Associate Professor at Buck County Community College in Newton, Pennsylvania:

"How come so many students ask about subliminal advertising?

It is an interesting, controversial subject that gets coverage every so often in the one publication that all my students are required to read: Advertising Age.

Also, the subject was featured in a fairly recent movie ('Agency,' starring Robert Mitchum and Lee Majors) that far too many of my students seemed to have viewed."

Another practitioner, Craig Astler, a copywriter with Zechman & Associates in Chicago, took me to task for having the nerve to suggest that advertising professionals denounce the suggestion that they embed subliminals:

> "Prof. Haberstroh's article on subliminal adver-
> tising was enlightening, but his plea for adpeople to
> speak out against such charges seems a little mis-
> guided. By doing so, we as ad professionals, will
> only add credence to Wilson Bryan Key's silly the-
> ories. Even worse, we'll make the public believe we
> have something to hide."

Michael Ward, a copywriter/broadcast producer operating out
of Baton Rouge, Louisiana, summed up his weariness with the
entire subject in his letter:

> "With rapidly diminishing interest, I have read
> the coverage in Ad Age on subliminal advertising.
> Of all the things I can think of to say on this subject,
> two words strike me as most to the point.
>
> So what.
>
> As an advertising creative, I know I don't do it.
> I also know nobody else does. And I know that if we
> did, it wouldn't work. We all know these things.
>
> Now I find your Viewpoint section is once again
> dominated by this hurricane in a highball glass. I
> have more important concerns. (A product benefit,
> for example, that needs to be phrased into a headline
> in a persuasive, concise and dramatic way.)
> Subliminals simply have nothing to do with my job.
> And I am beginning to wish that people would stop
> taking up space in a magazine that, otherwise, is rel-
> evant. When Ad Age published that first article, you
> seemed to have opened a door to a flood. This read-
> er's viewpoint?
>
> Close the door. Then lock it and throw away the
> Key."

Ted Richards, who publishes the "Effective Advertising
Newsletter in Rockford, Illinois, had this to say:

"I would like, reluctantly, to comment on Jack Haberstroh's article, "Can't ignore subliminal ad charges" (AA, Sept. 17). He asked why 'the advertising world remains silent in the face of Wilson Bryan Key's 'preposterous' and 'absurd' charges against the industry of using subliminal embeds.

Mr. Key's charges are virtually unanswerable. Just as if responding to 'When did you stop beating your wife?' you start in a hole (Whoops!) you never quite get out of. Mr. Key understands there is much more profit in writing and lecturing about voodoo and witchcraft than there is in its practice."

Of course Dr. Key himself refused to remain mute. He charged into the fracas, the first with a letter aimed at me:

"I am still overwhelmed, gratified, and even somewhat breathless over your Sept. 17 review of my three books...Jack Haberstroh's sparkling, cobra-tongued invective made my whole week — in spite of his frequent factual inaccuracies...I now feel my life is complete, my destiny fulfilled and my immortality assured.

Mr. Haberstroh's constant reiteration of indignant denials by ad executives ('adfolk,' as he terms them) on their knowledge of subliminal techniques must have reminded at least a few readers of that oft-quoted Shakespearean line 'Methinks thou dost protest too much' or that aged response from the chicken thief, 'Ain't nobody out here but us chickens.'

I really cannot comprehend Mr. Haberstroh's perceptual hangups. Most of the subliminal embeds in the three illustrations published with his piece are clearly evident, except for the Gilbey's ad which was cropped too close on the bottom, thereby eliminating the full genitalia display. I assume your picture editor attempted to protect Ad Age readers from overstimulating ideas.

I am also intrigued at Mr. Haberstroh's offhand conclusion that those many millions of individuals who read, seriously weighed and independently confirmed what I described in the books were mere gullible, foolish, mindless souls incapable of critical thought. Such a conclusion from an academic paid to propagandize for an $80 billion annual expenditure used to modify, manipulate and control consumer behavior is reminiscent of George Orwell's doublethink from his Ministry of Truth — 'War is Peace, Freedom is Slavery and Ignorance is Strength.'

But then, we hear a lot of similar rhetoric from the advertising media as they merchandise candidates during this election year 1984. Never forget the Sin in Sincere or the Con in Confidence."

Six weeks later he reloaded and fired. This time at Jock Elliott:

"In answer to the primitive wailings of Jock Elliott, Jr. (AA, Oct. 4) who would ban my books about subliminal advertising from university campuses and who wants the academic world to 'shut up' on the subject, his intemperate admonishments did more to confirm my data than anything in my three books. I have recently used Ogilvy & Mather ads in my lectures, perhaps explaining his rage. Mr. Elliott might enjoy testifying on the subject of subliminal advertising before the next congressional committee which delves into the area. All Jack Haberstroh's fact-thin article (AA, Sept. 17) proved was that some ad executives lie a lot. But then, we already knew this.

The late comedian, Lenny Bruce, once advised husbands that 'whenever your wife finds you in bed with another woman, never admit anything. Even if she has pictures,' he added, 'never admit anything!' Mr. Elliott knows, of course, that I have lots of pictures in each of my three books, as do my students and academic colleagues.

I would be delighted to debate Jock Elliott, or any other ad executive publicly on the subject of subliminal advertising any time or place he desires."

Few practitioners rallied publicly to my side. One of the very few was Leland Katz, in Marketing Communications at the Digital Equipment Corp., in Sharon, Massachusetts:

"It was with a mounting sense of anger that I read Jack Haberstroh's article on subliminal advertising (AA, Sept. 17). Anger, not at Jack, but at the need for the article's having to be written in the first place. And make no mistake, it had to be done.

I have been in this business for a long time...I have worked with at least a dozen advertising agencies and with countless independent and affiliated copywriters and art directors. I have never seen, nor have I known anyone who has seen, any deliberately embedded messages or symbols — sexual or otherwise. I can only conclude from the evidence provided in the article, that Mr. Key, who appears to be an intelligent man, based on his ability to lecture, write books, and obtain professional positions, knows precisely what he is doing; $270,000 per year in lecture fees alone can be a powerful motivating force."

A few supportive personal letters trickled in. One such was this flattering note from the highly respected Stavros Cosmopulos, Chairman of the Board of Cosmopulos, Crowley, & Daly of Boston:

"I enjoyed your article in the September 17th issue of Advertising Age. Whenever I speak or lecture the question of subliminal advertising invariably comes up, particularly at schools. In all the years that I have been on the creative side of this business I've never used subliminal anything in ads. Although I remember an illustrator tried to slip something through once (he got chewed out and was never used again). You are right the matter does need airing out.

From the tone of your article it sounds like you
are passing on to your students good solid information about advertising, a rare commodity these days
in communications courses. Good for you."

Another of this very small handful was from the Director of
Corporate Relations of the Kemper Group in Long Grove, Illinois:

"You deserve commendation for the research
you have done into subliminal advertising.

I teach a course at North Central College in
Naperville, Illinois, and I have had experiences similar to yours with students who have read books by
Wilson Bryan Key. In fact, his works have provided
the basis for some stimulating class discussions.

I agree with you that the advertising industry's
refusal to actively rebut his claims has given credence where no credence is due. Your work reveals
his books for what they are — rubbish that exemplifies the intellectual bankruptcy of some academics.

Would it be possible to get additional information on your survey, or does the Advertising Age
story contain all the available information?

Again, my congratulations on a needed and
worthwhile piece of work."

David Mink, Vice President of Club Services of the American
Advertising Federation, wrote a brief supportive note, calling subliminal embedding "a 'phantom' issue, devoid of practitioners."

This letter to me was penned by Jeff Atlas, a senior copywriter
at Ogilvy & Mather in New York:

"For years, I have been infuriated by Mr. Key's
charges of *Subliminal Seduction*. I was pleased to
read in Advertising Age that someone is attacking
these absurd, unfounded, and unsubstantiated lies.

I hope that my revulsion at his charges is apparent. If there is any way I can be of assistance to you please do not hesitate to let me know.

Perhaps you would like to put together some debate about this topic. If so, I would be pleased to attend.

It is an insult to everyone in this business that people believe his lies.

Of course, the real question is, why do so many people believe them?"

Hell, I even responded to my own article. My letter, and a reproduction of the September 17th, 1984 cover art (Fig. 17), ran in Ad Age on October 22nd:

"Yesterday one of my students told me she is also taking a Psychology of Advertising class in our College of Business. Naturally, they discuss subliminals

The professor teaching the class made copies of my (Sept. 17) Ad Age article for every member of the class. Then, they spent a significant portion of a class period finding all the "SEXes" which your artist deliberately placed in the cover art!

Specifically they found "SEXes" under the drawing table, on the right; on the illustration tacked to the wall; on the artist's trousers. Hell, all over the place in that piece of artwork!

C'mon, Ad Age. Did the artist 'do it?' Or didn't he (she)?

You gotta tell me."

I signed my name, calling myself the "Pervert Professor."

The "Viewpoint" Editor responded to the jibe on the same page:

"College students should not be reduced

> to looking for "SEX" on an Ad Age cover.
> Says artist Tom Herzberg: 'That's fantastic.
> Gee, no I didn't. It must have all been sub-
> conscious. I didn't know I was that good.'"

Two or three other professors wrote — one offering me a teaching position at his large university — and then it was Advertising
Age's turn.

The publication probably summed up the feeling of the majority of practitioners in its September 24th editorial. Its conclusion:

> "As we understand it, remaining mute, in this
> instance, only means that advertising professionals
> have better things to do with their time. The gullible
> will always be among us. And so will the likes of
> Mr. Key, who is, if nothing else, a past master at
> feeding the fantasies of the gullible."

Sid Bernstein, former Chairman of the Executive Committee of
Crain Communications, chimed in with this personal note to me at
the time:

> "I am pleased that you have been talking to col-
> lege students about the non-existence of subliminal
> advertising...I should think you would be a wel-
> come speaker at advertising clubs, and suggest you
> let the advertising Federation of America know of
> your availability if you have not already done so.
> You might write to Howard Bell...and tell him I
> suggested you get in touch with him, if you want
> to."

Of course I wrote to Mr. Bell immediately, though the ad club
response was hardly overwhelming. In the seven years since my
letter to Bell, only four ad clubs have contacted me, and I've spo-
ken at three. Two in Missouri. One in Arizona.

In another personal letter, Bernstein took me to task for my
hyperbolic comment that "advertising publications report nothing"
about subliminal advertising. The fact is, in a thousand years of
writing a weekly column for Advertising Age, Bernstein only
devoted two of them to the subject. He chastised the ad business in

1978 for <u>not</u> speaking out on the subject of subliminal advertising, as I did six years later:

> "...no one seems to be able to explain why advertisers trying to sell shoes or sealing wax, or telephone service would want to louse up their expensive ad messages with corny or dirty subliminal messages. But it isn't funny, and <u>everyone in advertising should do everything possible to knock this subliminal nonsense right out of the box every chance he gets</u>." (my underlining)

Apparently Bernstein forgot his admonition — or felt that he alone had the right to rebuke the ad industry — for five years later he seemed to have changed his "company line." In an Ad Age column in May, 1983, headlined "Stop beating this dead horse!", Bernstein took advertising professors to task. He acknowledged that "not one of them believes there is such a thing as 'subliminal' advertising."

> "So why this grand passion for continuing discussions of it and research efforts devoted to it? <u>Why not let this phony horse die the ignoble death</u> it so richly deserves, instead of constantly thinking up new research aspects to prove that no advertiser is idiot enough to waste money on it." (my underlining)

Later in the same column he calls for a halt to research and discussions of the subject by the American Academy of Advertising members (educators in advertising and related subjects):

> "All you do is perpetuate the notion that such advertising does exist — with the obvious result that more and more students (and others) are led to believe that <u>all this attention proves the contention that it in fact does exist</u> and practitioners are frantically trying to hide the truth from a gullible public." (my underlining)

Apparently Bernstein, who wrote a weekly column for "Crain's

International Newspaper of Marketing" (Ad Age), took his <u>1983</u> advice. Unless I'm badly mistaken, he never devoted another column since that date to the subject of subliminal advertising.

The mass media, on the other hand, have had a field day with the subject. And interest — particularly among bright, young, well-educated individuals — continues to grow. In the year following my Ad Age article I was invited to appear on more than forty radio call-in talk shows.

One of them was an exhausting three-hour debate with Dr. Key over WNWS in Miami. The talk show producer later called it a "fantastic" show. Incoming calls were backed up all evening long.

By the summer of 1991 I had expected interest in the subject to have waned. As a spokesperson for the House of Seagram and their wonderful subliminal spoof magazine campaign for Seagram's Gin (Figs. 18, 19, 20), I was again on the TV and talk-show circuit. Invariably callers were kept on hold as switchboards lit up with incoming calls. Most callers "knew" they had seen embeds, or had "heard" them.

The public's fascination with the subject has never diminished. On the contrary. A greater percentage of Americans believe that professionals are constantly embedding subliminal messages in advertising...than ever before!

An excellent nationwide survey of 800 American adults, selected at random, was published in May, 1991 by Response Analysis Corp., based in Princeton, New Jersey. The research firm found that 62% of American adults believe that advertising professionals are continuously embedding subliminal messages in the advertising they create.

Last time I counted there are more subliminal advertising believers than registered Republicans!

Chapter 6

How do you <u>know</u> so many believe it?

Chapter 6

How do you <u>know</u> so many believe it?

Who in the world, advertising professionals ask, would ever believe such titillating tomfoolery?

The answer is...unfortunately...<u>most</u> Americans!

The number of Americans who believe that advertising agency artists are laboriously painting women's nipples, bleeding penises, skulls, scorpions, and the word "fuck" into advertising artwork seems to be steadily increasing over the decades. In May, 1958, less than two years after Vicary's movie theater experiments — and his coining the term "subliminal advertising" — Ralph Haber, a researcher at Stanford, found 41% of his sample of San Franciscans, knew about the phenomenon.

In May of 1991, three decades and four books by Dr. Key later, nearly two-thirds of all U.S. adults believe advertising agency professionals are sketching subliminals into virtually all the advertising art their agency produces!

Nearly as many adult Americans think advertising artists are actively doing it as believe there's life after death!

A major research study on the subject was commissioned by the House of Seagram's in the Spring of 1991.

The research was conducted during the second week of April, 1991 by Response Analysis in Princeton, New Jersey. Data was gathered by telephone, using a national probability sample of 800 U.S. adults. I assisted in the question formulation, and later in the data analysis. The results are subject to a margin of error of three percentage points.

Less than thirty-five years after subliminal advertising experiments were first conducted in this country, Response Analysis found that 62% of all U.S. adults think subliminal messages are being constantly and deliberately embedded in the nation's advertising.

Most Americans, they found, think subliminal advertising can get them to buy things they don't want to buy.

The research also discovered a high degree of correlation between youth and belief in intentionally embedding messages — i.e. the younger you are the more likely you are to believe advertising artists are inserting subliminals in agency artwork.

Armed with the results, Seagram's Extra Dry Gin would later launch its "Hidden Pleasures" magazine campaign which spoofed subliminal advertising in a light-hearted, "fun" way. Readers of Seagram's Gin ads in national magazines would be asked, for instance, to find an easily identifiable (and clothed) couple on a swing in the bubbles of a gin-and-tonic. Or a golfer etc. with, of course, help from a tiny arrow. (Figs. 18, 19, 20)

Response Analysis found a positive correlation between youth and the likelihood of believing that you'll find subliminals in your advertising.

Believability by Age Category that Subliminals Are Used

54% of those 55 or older
60% of 35-54 year-olds
62% of 25-34 year-olds
69% of 21-24 year-olds

Clearly, the younger one is, the more likely it is that he or she will believe that advertising practitioners are embedding subliminals in advertising artwork.

The study also found that young adults were far more likely than older individuals to believe that subliminal messages in advertising could force them to buy something they did not want to purchase.

Subliminals Can Force Me to Buy, by Age Category

45% of those 55 or older
58% of 35-54 year-olds
58% of 25-34 year-olds
66% of 21-24 year-olds

This, despite substantial evidence that subliminal messages have no effect whatsoever on consumer buying behavior.

Almost 80% of the country's "senior citizens" think the use of subliminals in advertising is unethical. Younger respondents generally found their use more acceptable — despite their feelings that subliminals will more often force them to make purchases they really don't want to make.

Subliminals Are Ethical, by Age Category

21% of those 55 or older
23% of 35-54 year-olds
25% of 25-34 year-olds
40% of 21-24 year-olds

This same study — remember it was commissioned by the House of Seagram — found that campaigns which spoofed subliminals (like Seagram's Extra Dry Gin) were well liked, particularly by young adults.

Enjoy Subliminal Spoof Campaigns, by Age Category

37% of those 55 or older
53% of 35-54 year-olds
55% of 25-34 year-olds
65% of 21-24 year-olds

"People want to believe advertisers are putting subliminal messages in their ads," commented Jim Barrett, senior product manager for Seagram's Gin. "Our new spoof ads gently tap into that belief to involve our audiences in a fun and interactive way," he said shortly after the survey completion.

John O'Toole, president of the 4As, issued this response to the Response Analysis 1991 survey:

"The great percentage of adults who believe subliminal ads are used is frustrating. People seem to want to believe there is a conspiracy on the part of advertisers. But there is no conspiracy. Advertisers don't practice subliminal advertising."

The research confirmed many of the findings of earlier subliminal advertising awareness studies. Particularly the meticulous 1988 research by Synodinos; and Zanot's exacting 1983 study. Especially interesting is the high degree of correlation among all three studies on age and educational demographic characteristics. That is, generally speaking, the younger and better educated you are, the more likely you are to believe that ad agency practitioners are doing a subliminal number on your brain. And that's got to be bad news for the advertising industry! Instead of the whole monstrous myth melting away, like some orgy-filled ice cube, more and more young, well educated individuals are buying into Dr. Key's dipsy doo-doo.

An even more recent study was published in the Journal of Advertising Research in 1993. Brilliantly conducted by Bowling Green State University professors Martha Rogers and Kirk H. Smith, the study confirms all earlier studies in the very high percentage of Americans who believe that advertisers are using subliminal techniques. And in correlating age and education with belief in advertisers and their agencies using such techniques.

Rogers and Smith confined their research to the adult population of the city of Toledo, Ohio. A sample of 400 was obtained by telephone. 74.3% had heard of subliminal advertising — similar to the 81.3% reported by Zanot, and the 76% which Synodinos reported.

61.5% said they believed advertisers were placing "subliminal messages in advertisements or use this technology." Again, there is a high degree of correlation with earlier studies. Rogers and Smith put it this way:

> "Each study covered slightly different ground. Each was subject to different limitations, yet all three produced similar findings, despite the demographic variations of their populations.
>
> All three surveys found similar proportions who were aware of subliminal advertising, who believed that it is used by advertisers, and who thought that it 'works' to help sell products. It is reasonable to assume that widespread belief in subliminal advertising is a national phenomenon."

Certainly the most exacting — and statistically sophisticated — study of public belief in subliminal advertising was that carried out by the brilliant Nicolaos Synodinos in 1988 in the City and County of Honolulu. The research was aided by a faculty grant from the College of Business Administration at the University of Hawaii. 500 adult residents of the City and County of Honolulu were selected via a random digit dialing (RDD) method.

Synodinos calls the similarities between his study and Zanot's 1983 research "remarkable." Like Zanot, Synodinos found the public believing that subliminals are being widely and frequently used in advertising. His findings also concur with a 1985 study by Block and Vanden Bergh that found that as education increased, subjects found subliminals more and more unethical. And professionals, for instance, were more likely than non-professionals to find the use of subliminal advertising unethical.

Block and Vanden Bergh also found that most consumers were skeptical about the effectiveness of subliminal self-improvement tapes. Those most likely to buy subliminal self-help tapes were less affluent, less well educated, and perhaps experiencing family problems.

Synodinos concluded his study with this warning to the advertising industry:

> "The advertising community has to educate the public about the myths surrounding the topic because such a reliance can become a dangerous proposition: During the last 30 years several attempts have been made in the United States and in other countries to regulate the 'evil' practice of 'subliminal advertising' despite the lack of scientific evidence of its use and effectiveness."

Of course advertising agencies were just as deaf to his 1988 warning as they were to my pleading in 1984.

In 1989 I supervised two small research studies which dealt with the public perception of subliminal advertising. Their unique demographics suggest they may not be applicable to large publics.

The first of the two surveys was designed to determine the perception of subliminals in the predominantly black city of Richmond, Virginia and its surrounding counties.

Conducted in March, 1989, individuals were randomly selected from the greater Richmond C & P Telephone Directory. 184 usable telephone interviews were conducted.

Most individuals, as we suspected, had heard of subliminal advertising.

> 61.7% had heard of it
> 38.3% had not heard of it

We asked the respondents who had heard about it, whether or not they thought advertisers were using subliminals.

Again, as we expected, most thought most advertising contains subliminals. Nearly three out of four believed that advertisers were intentionally implanting unperceived messages.

> 70.7% think advertisers are using sublimi-
> nals in their advertising
> 29.3% do not think advertisers are using
> subliminals in their advertising

I was also curious about how often the public thinks advertisers use subliminal techniques. The answers came back as follows:

Very Often	17.7%
Often	26.6%
Sometimes	33.9%
Seldom	11.3%
Never	10.5%

(Very Often + Often) } 44.3%
(Very Often + Often + Sometimes) } 78.2%

Almost one of five respondents felt that advertisers are using subliminal techniques "Very Often." That would suggest their rather complete agreement with Dr. Key's view that one "cannot pick up a newspaper, magazine, or pamphlet, hear radio, or view television anywhere in North America etc." without being barraged by subliminals. Almost half of the respondents thought advertisers use subliminals "often" or "very often." Again, the finding suggests respondents thought subliminals are very liberally sprinkled over a wide range of media.

Like Response Analysis two years later, we were also interested in whether or not respondents considered the use of such subliminals "acceptable and ethical."

More than half of all our respondents felt the use of subliminal techniques was not acceptable, nor was it ethical. Here are the results of our "acceptable/ethical" question:

> 21.4%   felt using subliminals is acceptable and ethical
>
> 51.6%   felt using subliminals is not acceptable nor ethical
>
> 27.0%   had no opinion

A second survey on the same subject, which I also supervised in 1989, was even more limited in scope. I was particularly curious about how an "educated" audience — an academic community of faculty and students on a university campus, for instance — would react to the two most important questions in the March, 1989 study. We put the questions this way:

> (1) Do you believe most advertising contains subliminal messages?
>
> (2) Do you think subliminal advertising is an honest or dishonest way to sell a product?

This study was conducted by one of my students, Jaggi Khandelwal, on the two campuses of Virginia Commonwealth University in Richmond, during May, 1989.

He distributed 224 printed questionnaires to students and faculty throughout the university., In each instance he waited for the individual to read the simple explanation of subliminal advertising, and answer the two questions above. The explanation:

Subliminal Advertising

"Subliminal advertising is a form of advertising which assumes only the subconscious can comprehend it. An example of a subliminal message might occur in a movie theater where the message 'Popcorn' may appear many times on the screen, but no one can see it since it flashes too fast to be consciously seen."

Almost 51% of this small, but "highly educated" group of respondents believed that most advertising does, indeed, contain subliminal messages. And nearly two-thirds of them felt it's a dishonest way to sell a product. Here are the data:

(1) Do you believe most advertising contains subliminal messages

	%	(N)
Yes	50.9	114
No	36.2	81
Don't Know/ No opinion	12.9	29

(2) Do you think subliminal advertising is an honest or dishonest way to sell a product?

	%	(N)
Honest	17.4	39
Dishonest	64.3	144
Don't Know/ No opinion	18.3	41

We are, of course, creatures of our own perceptions. Whether or not there really are deliberately embedded subliminals lurking in advertising art, in one sense, is unimportant. If our perception is that they are present, for instance, we will act upon that perception. Whether or not it corresponds with reality.

An earlier study of the public's perception of subliminals — and a very good one — was conducted by telephone in the Washington D.C. and surrounding areas. It was sponsored by the Center for Research in Public Communication at the College of

Journalism at the University of Maryland. Heading up the research team was the highly regarded Dr. Eric J. Zanot of the College of Journalism at the University of Maryland. Assisting him were J. David Pincus and E. Joseph Lamb, doctoral candidates at the University of Maryland. Their detailed study appeared in The Journal of Advertising in 1983.

A total of 209 telephone interviews were conducted using names randomly selected from directories for Washington D.C., northern Virginia, and suburban Maryland.

81% (170) had heard of subliminal advertising. And, of that group, 81% (144) answered "yes" to the following question:

> "Some people believe that advertisers intention-
> ally place a hidden message or messages that you
> are not consciously aware of in their advertisements.
> These 'subliminal messages' are designed to per-
> suade you to buy the product, even though you may
> not be aware that the hidden message is in the ad.
> Have you ever heard of this advertising technique?"

Another 12% were uncertain.

68% (122) of those who had heard of the phenomenon believe that subliminal advertising assists in the selling of products. And most respondents, 51% (90), think that advertisers use subliminal techniques "always" or "often" when asked the question:

> "How often do you believe subliminal advertis-
> ing is used?"

The Zanot study concludes:

> "Public awareness of the phenomenon of sub-
> liminal advertising is widespread and has increased
> over the past two decades. Approximately 78% of
> the subjects in this study stated that they knew what
> subliminal advertising is...Respondents believe that
> subliminal advertising is widely and frequently used
> and that it is successful in selling product. They also
> tend to believe it is an unacceptable, unethical, and
> harmful advertising technique. Many respondents

state these beliefs would affect their buying behavior if they thought a particular advertiser were using
subliminal techniques...The individual most likely
to have heard of subliminal advertising is white,
well-educated (at least some college), with a rela-
tively high income (over $20,000 per year)."

Ralph Haber, a research associate in the Institute for
Communication Research at Stanford at the time, conducted one of
the only other studies on the public's perception of subliminal
advertising. This was back in 1959.

The renowned Wilbur Schramm, former director of the School
of Journalism at the University of Iowa — and founder of its cele-
brated Writers' Workshop — directed the research study. Haber
added questions about subliminal advertising to a much larger
questionaire about the spread of scientific knowledge.

324 interviews were conducted in San Francisco during the second and third weeks of May, 1958. The two questions of interest to
our subject were:

"Have you heard of the possibility of using
advertising on TV where the ads would be so dim,
or flashed so fast, that you would not be aware of
them being there? (This is called subliminal advertising)

(If 'yes' to No. 1) "Do you feel there is anything
unethical or wrong with this kind of advertising?"

41% of his sample indicated they had heard of subliminal
advertising. 49% of the males in the sample, but only 34% of the
females, had heard of it.

Haber concluded that those who had heard of the phenomenon
were more likely to be male, younger, and better educated in general, and..."had taken more science classes."

His respondents were evenly split on the ethics of subliminal
advertising. 50% claimed it was ethical, 50% found it unethical.

Chapter 7

<u>Why</u> are there so many believers?

Chapter 7

Why are there so many believers?

First of all, as we've seen in the last chapter, most Americans are believers. They believe that those of us in advertising are actually — painstakingly — embedding subliminal messages and objects in our advertising artwork.

The Response Analysis 1991 survey, for instance, found that 62% of all U.S. adults believe that advertisers are intentionally embedding communications below the perception threshold.

62% — that's a higher percentage of American adults than the percentage who admit they're Protestant!

While professionals and professors pooh-pooh the whole idea, the public's buying Dr. Key's kooky accusations. It's intrigued — fascinated — by what it can "find" in ice cube artwork. On Parkay patties, Horsman doll clothing, Ritz crackers, Howard Johnson placemats, and in the swirling gunk of a sink, suddenly liberated for a TV commercial, by lascivious Liquid-Plumr.

Clearly, the vast majority of Americans perceive the advertiser — and particularly the ad agency practitioner — to be a conniver. As a sneaky pitchman with few, if any, scruples. And the younger and better educated you are, the more likely you are to feel that way!

But why? Why do so many feel this way about advertising professionals? And why do so very many believe those same advertising professionals are embedding subliminal nonsense to sell goods and services?

One reason is the coverage the mass media have given the subject. Many of the news stories about subliminal messages fail to mention conflicting negative evidence. As Pratkanis and Aronson point out in their Age of Propaganda:

"When disconfirming evidence is presented, it is

usually near the end of the article, giving the reader
the impression that, at worst, the claims for subliminal effectiveness are somewhat controversial."

As I stated in chapter 2, "Who Started It?" the concept began in
1957 as a fraud. Daily newspapers from coast to coast reported
Vicary's claims that popcorn and Coke sales jumped 58% and 18%,
respectively, due to the subliminal implants he embedded in a
movie.

When he repeated the experiment, and it failed to produce any
increases in popcorn and Coke sales, the media, strangely, fell
silent. Advertising Age alone reported the fiasco, and Vicary's subsequent recantation.

Indeed, from the moment of its contaminated conception, newspapers have given negative evidence for the existence of subliminals very little ink. Television and radio continue to provide readily available forums for Dr. Key's nutty notions. Even in the world
of research, studies disproving the effectiveness of subliminal
advertising rarely seem to generate the publicity that pro-embed
research does.

Secondly, the public wants to believe ad guys are bad guys! The
public has consistently ranked advertising practitioners near the
very bottom of a list of 24 occupations in Gallup's every-other-year
"ethics and honesty" surveys. A nationwide sample was asked:

"How would you rate the honesty and ethical
standards of people in these different fields — very
high, high, average, low, or very low."

The five occupations receiving the lowest, or worst, scores
were,: state political officeholders, insurance salesmen, labor union
leaders, advertising practitioners, and car salesmen. Collectively,
the survey reveals, occupations that involve selling receive the
lowest scores. Only one person in ten rates the ethics of realtors,
insurance salesmen, advertising practitioners, and auto salesmen in
positive terms.

A 1985 nationwide survey of focus groups in five cities, and
responses to more than 1,000 questionnaires, reveals much the
same findings as the bi-annual Gallup studies. Commissioned by

the American Society of Newspaper Editors, respondents were asked the following question:

> "Please rate the honesty and ethical standards of people in each of these occupations."

Ten occupations were listed. Again, advertising executives were ranked next to the bottom, just above used-car salesmen.

In one sense, this "conspiracy theory" which finds the practice of advertising one of the least moral occupations in the country, is surprising.

Surprising, because advertising's primary purpose — its raison d'etre — is to sell goods and services for clients. Often, to enhance the image of a brand, increase its awareness, improve its bottom line. Yet, it hasn't been able to do this for itself.

Despite the fact that no occupation spends as much energy polishing its own tawdry image, overwhelming its practitioners with superfluous awards, canonizing its constituents, and inducting its long-of-tooth into silly Halls of Fame.

Why, I suspect the public reasons, is it so difficult to believe that these advertising charlatans — engaged as they are in all sorts of unethical and dishonest activities — are embedding subliminal messages and objects? I can imagine an "average" citizen thinking that implanting a four-letter word in an advertisement, which couldn't be read or seen, isn't nearly as evil as selling things to children. That practice was forbidden by the Code of Hammurabi 4,000 years ago, under the penalty of death. Or portraying women as sex objects, or household drudges. Or polluting the environment with hundreds of thousands of advertising billboards. Or flat-out lying to the public about the structural integrity of an automobile, secretly strengthening its frame while cutting the frames of competing cars in a strength comparison experiment for a television commercial. Or putting marbles in a bowl of soup, so it'll appear to TV cameras that the "vegetable" soup is simply loaded with yummy vegetables. And the list goes on. And on.

If the advertising industry doesn't realize by now it has one hell of an image problem...what more can I say? Most citizens equate advertising practitioners with snake-oil hucksters. The majority of

Americans feel advertising makes them buy things they don't want to buy.

Pratkanis and Aronson discuss a third reason the concept of intentionally embedded subliminals is so believable. The idea of subliminally transmitted messages appeared in widely read media in the mid-50s, just a few years after the Korean War.

That war introduced the world to "brainwashing" and hypnotic suggestion. For the first time in the history of warfare, a nation was able to turn its prisoners of war against one another on a massive scale. True, the death rate for captured Americans was higher than for any war Americans had ever fought. The Defense Department released the following figures: of a total of 7,190 American prisoners, 2,730 died in captivity.

Nevertheless, twenty-one American captives voluntarily decided to remain with the enemy — an unheard of event; and more than one out of every three captured Americans in Korea was guilty of collaboration with the enemy.

The methods used by the Chinese to indoctrinate and "brainwash" American captives are meticulously related in J.A.C. Brown's first-rate Techniques of Persuasion. Americans saw, and read about for the first time, the apparently successful use of "mind-bending" techniques. Methods with which most Americans were unfamiliar.

Vicary's timing of his subliminal movie theater experiments, a short four years after the end of the Korean War, was near-perfect. While specific "brainwashing" techniques used by the Chinese against American prisoners were unknown to most Americans, U.S. citizens knew "something" strange had happened to U.S. prisoners of war. Something new and mysterious.

Perhaps, Americans thought, Vicary's experiments had validity. After all, if the Chinese could "persuade" more than a third of all the Americans they had captured to collaborate with the enemy, perhaps there's something to these subliminal messages of Vicary's.

And the Chinese were able to indoctrinate our prisoners very quickly. Only four days after the war began, an American officer who had been in captivity only 48 hours, broadcast the following message over Seoul radio:

> "Dear friends, we, all prisoners, solidly appeal to you as follows: the armed intervention in Korean internal affairs is quite a barbaristic (sic) aggressive action to protect the benefit of the capitalist monopolists of the U.S.A. Let us fight for right against wrong, bravely opposing to be mobilized into such a war against Russia."

Later the Chinese released small groups of "brainwashed" American captives. These individuals brought with them letters which they, and fellow prisoners, had written protesting the war. Similar letters from American prisoners began appearing all over the world in pro-Communist newspapers.

America was ripe for Vicary. And any mind-altering methods.

Of course, Dr. Wilson Bryan Key revived the idea in the 70s. This time big business and their advertising agencies were the oul prits.

Pratkanis and Aronson speculate about the ready acceptance today of subliminal imprints:

> "Today, there appears to be a growing tendency to turn to quick-fix, Rambo-like solutions to complex problems, whether these solutions be trillion-dollar defense systems in the sky or $14.95 subliminal cassette tapes designed to improve painlessly our self-esteem. Our theories of what should be may have caused us to be too uncritical of claims for the power of subliminal influence."

Another reason for the widespread belief in the existence of intentionally embedded subliminal messages might be called the "devil made me do it" theory."

Response Analysis, in their 1991 Seagram's sponsored nationwide survey, uncovered this spurious reason for belief in subliminals.

800 adult Americans were asked whether or not subliminal advertising could get them to purchase products they did not want to buy. On average, 56% believed it could!

Interestingly, the younger you are, the more likely you are to believe subliminal advertising will influence you personally.

One can easily imagine the shopper, her arms piled high with expensive items she had just purchased at the mall, telling her husband "I just couldn't help it! It was all those subliminal messages mixed in with the music in that department store! Yep, I just couldn't help myself! Honey, I had to buy all this stuff!"

And, while we're at it, let's give the "devil" his due. Dr. Wilson Bryan Key has done a marvelous selling job, promoting subliminals and their effectiveness. Almost single-handedly — oh, add Hal Becker and a gaggle of self-help tape hustlers — he has kept the myth alive. He's appeared on almost every radio and TV talk-show imaginable. He crisscrosses the country constantly, giving thirty to forty paid and sold-out lectures on college campuses every year. He's authored four books. Though some say it's the same book, rewritten three times. But the fact is, they sell well — about two million copies at last count.

Sid Dudley, a marketing professor at East Carolina University, agrees. He gives Dr. Key most of the credit for the continuing popularity of the subliminal myth. Writing in a 1987 issue of the Akron Business and Economic Review, he claims that "Key's books, combined with his personal appearances, are largely responsible for the public's belief in the power of subliminal suggestion."

I've known Dr. Key personally since 1974. Though neither I, nor any of my professional colleagues, buy a single ounce of what he's selling, he is quite believable nonetheless. He comes across in guest lectures in my college classrooms as enthusiastic, knowledgeable, and very believable. Though I would repudiate his theories point-by-point beforehand, a large percentage of my advertising students found themselves believing there's a lot more than clams on the clam-plate!

Evidence for that came in the form of two surveys I gave my advertising students at San Diego State University in 1974. Even though we had thoroughly discussed subliminal advertising in each section of my Introductory Advertising class. And I felt I had conscientiously invalidated Dr. Key's claims that most advertising is being intentionally embedded. The survey results were, nevertheless, a surprise.

Students filled out the survey only if they had been present at Dr. Key's guest lecture of October 30th, 1974. Here's the survey, and its surprising results:

> Fill out ONLY if you attended Dr. Wilson Key's presentation last Thursday (Oct. 30th) at 11 a.m. in SS-258.

> (Place a check-mark next to the statement that most clearly approximates your feelings about Dr. Key's assertions.)

(N)	%	
27	20.0	The majority of artists and photographers and others involved in the creation of advertising are deliberately placing subliminal words and symbols in advertising.
36	26.7	Roughly half of the artists and photographers and others involved in the creation of advertising are deliberately placing subliminal words and symbols in advertising.
69	51.1	Extremely few artists and photographers and others involved in the creation of advertising are deliberately placing subliminal words and symbols in advertising.
3	2.2	No artist or photographers or other individual involved in the creation of advertising would ever deliberately place subliminal words and symbols in advertising.

135 100.0

The surprise was, of course, the large number of students —
remember, these were advertising students, many of whom were
planning on a career in that industry — who believe that most
advertising artists and photographers are intentionally embedding
subliminals. This, after a thorough discounting of Dr. Key's theories in my classrooms prior to Dr. Key's appearance.

But the principal reason for the rejuvenation of the subliminal
myth, and its increasing popularity with the American public, is the
almost utter — and inexplicable — silence of the advertising industry.

No advertising practitioner I know has ever embedded anything
in artwork. Nor knows of anyone else in advertising who did. No
advertising educator I know — with perhaps one exception —
believes that embedding is taking place at a conscious, deliberate
level.

Yet two-thirds of the American public believes that those of us
who work professionally in advertising are spending incredible
numbers of hours, loading up artwork with messages, genitalia, and
orgies that no one can see!

Like the rest of the advertising world, when Dr. Key's first book
appeared in 1973, I found his ideas so ludicrous that I said or wrote
little about them. I knew they'd disappear quickly.

And so did my professional and professorial advertising colleagues. While Dr. Key began making the talk-show circuit, and
kicked off his enthusiastic campus crusade — aided by a barrage of
favorable newspaper and magazine pieces — we sat on our hands.
We knew — oh, we were so sure — it would soon disappear. Like
the flasher Dr. Key finds in your cocktail, he'll dissolve when the
ice melts.

But he didn't disappear. Thousands of us were wrong. He and
his sexy sappery became more popular than ever. In 1984
Advertising Age published a 4,000-word cover piece in which I
pleaded with the professional advertising community to speak out
— to deny any embedding was taking place.

I appeared on scores of talk shows, spoke to advertising clubs,
and wrote articles for other publications — imploring my professional advertising colleagues to get off their hands and take an

active part in discrediting Dr. Key and his whacko accusations. I chastised practitioners in the concluding paragraph of my 1984 Ad Age article:

> "While many advertising professionals sit mutely — and advertising publications report nothing about the issue — Mr. Key is in the hustings making converts by the thousands. It is an issue about which we must no longer remain mute."

The reaction to the article is described elsewhere in this book. If anything, I may have unwittingly belittled Dr. Key's power of conversion. I suspect he converted millions rather than thousands to his fatuous philosophy.

And, for the past ten years, Ad Age, the biggest advertising publication in the world, has been literally speechless on the subject of subliminal advertising. Is it any wonder two-thirds of all Americans think advertising professionals, and their cheer-leading press, have "something to hide?" Other advertising and media publications: AD Week, Editor & Publisher, Broadcasting, Communication Arts, Sales & Marketing Management, and Graphic Design, have all chosen to ignore the subject of subliminals.

In 1987 John O'Toole became president of the American Association of Advertising Agencies. One of his first formal actions was to terminate a study being conducted for the AAAA on the perception of subliminal advertising by the American public. "Why waste energy on a nonexistent phenomenon?" he said at the time. New York Magazine reported the debate between Dr. Key and advertising professionals in an excellent article written by Bernice Kanner, and published in its December 4th, 1989 issue. She concludes her piece with this comment from O'Toole:

> "Periodically, Key rehashes his ideas and tells the public that someone out there is trying to manipulate their minds. Subliminal suggestion may exist in psychological studies; it does not exist in advertising. People don't walk around in a semi-trance; buying is a rational, cognitive process. How can showing someone a penis get them to switch, say, from Kent to Marlboro? Seems to me that getting

people sexually aroused makes it harder, not easier
to sell them something."

And so, the industry that educates us to consume, for whatever
reason, has chosen not to educate the American public about the
sappiness of subliminals. The same industry that popularized Max
Headroom has "better things to do with its (their) time." The same
industry that remains mute about Willie Horton in a presidential
advertising campaign, now remains mute about hidden messages in
every ad we see and hear! And two-thirds of the public believe
they're there, and advertising professionals deliberately put them
there!

This little book — this one book — can't convert those millions who believe embeds have infected every commercial and ad
they're likely to ever perceive. No, advertising practitioners must,
at every opportunity, educate the public in the creative and effective
manner for which that institution has rightfully won a place in our
social history — to the silliness of subliminal advertising. For their
own sake. And for the continued — though lessened — believability of an institution that has been rightfully called "the most fun you
can have with your clothes on."

It won't be easy. Two-thirds of all Americans have willfully
accepted Dr. Key's baptism in baloney and have spread his gospel-
of-the-absurd from one corner of this country to the other. To para-
phrase Lewis Lapham in dispelling a perception "it is all but useless to assert anything so subversive as a fact." No, you'll have to
do better than that. It'll take a massive amount of enthusiastic siz-
zle-selling.

To my colleagues in the "real" world of advertising: of course
you waited too long to speak out. You waited until Dr. Key had
made "believers" out of most Americans! I'm not too modest to
suggest that I may have been right ten years ago...and the whole
damn advertising community wrong! For ten long years you said
hardly a word about subliminals. You just sat there on your hands
and let the public believe you were inserting all those male and
female fixtures in the ads and commercials you've been creating.
No wonder they believe you're guilty. You never once denied it.
Not once — that I know of — in ten long years!

For the sake of the institution in which you work, and its continuing effectiveness. And for the sake of those of us — thousands of us — who instruct curious and creative minds in advertising, preparing those minds for the dynamic and successful careers they'll find in that field...

...please deny the existence of subliminals every chance you get!

Chapter 8

Is it <u>legal</u>?

Chapter 8

Is it <u>legal</u>?

Yes. And no.

It's not illegal in print. You may, if you wish, embed all the male and female reproductive organs you wish in newspaper and magazine advertisements. Yeah, splash them all over billboards and direct mail pieces. There is no law, or postal regulation, forbidding the practice. You may airbrush photographs, etch printing plates, and use doctored acetate overlays in ingenious ways to slip your subliminal message into any print medium. Who's going to know whether or not there's a subliminal message there? Or when it appeared? Or whether or not anyone "saw" it?

Want to take the time and money — in your print ad — to draw the 150 occupants of the menagerie Dr. Key finds in a Calvert cocktail advertisement in a 1971 Playboy? Scorpions, mice, wolves, fish, rats, lizards, birds, swans, and cats? Be my guest. It ain't illegal.

Nobody'll see 'em. So how can anyone file a complaint against you? And, if they did, when was their mind "bent?" Where did the occurrence take place? Were you harmed in any way? Were there any witnesses to this ghastly event?

No, it's not illegal in print advertising. A number of anti-subliminal laws have been introduced. None have been passed.

The American Bar Association admits "the legal ramification of subliminal messages is hazy."

And a Nevada judge ruled that subliminal advertising is not protected by the first amendment to the constitution in the so-called "Free Speech" clause. But again, if it can't be perceived — heard or seen — what's to protect?

On December 10, 1982 Assemblyman Phillip Wyman (R-Bakersfield) introduced to the California Legislature a bill (No.

100) that would have required notification to individuals about to
be subjected to any subliminal messages in a public place. Violators
could receive fines up to $1,000.

The wording "This material contains subliminal embedding"
would have to be carried by any material in which its author had
inserted hidden messages.

Wyman felt that subliminal communication constituted an invasion of privacy, and viewed such messages as unethical and deceptive.

The ACLU disagreed, feeling that such action might "chill"
speech. That organization preferred that any such litigation be han-
dled by the California state attorney general's office as a fraud
against consumers. Marjorie Swartz, legislative advocate for the
ACLU in its California office, said at the time:

> "We don't know if it's a problem; it's a potential
> problem."

Despite the opposition of the ACLU and various advertising
organizations, the bill passed in the Assembly in June, 1983.

In a letter I received almost a year later, Dr. Key wrote that the
California State Senate Judiciary Committee was "amending it to
death — seven amendments so far."

He was right, the bill languished in the Judiciary Committee
until November 30, 1984 when it breathed its last.

As of this writing there is no federal or state law that prohibits
the embedding of subliminal messages or objects in print advertising.

A Yale constitutional law professor thinks the major problem in
generating a legal policy on subliminal communication and advertising is that it's too tough to define:

> "There is always a problem with definition. If
> we could agree on what it was, I would have little
> trouble suggesting it be banned."

Some feel, of course, that it is a deceptive advertising practice, forbidden by the Wheeler-Lea Amendments to the Federal Trade Commission Act. Section V of that Act reads:

> "Unfair and deceptive acts or practices in commerce are declared unlawful.:

> Section 5, FTC Act, 15, U.S.C., 45 (a) (1) (1970)

The FTC could clearly squash any subliminal embedding — if it were being done — but obviously has chosen not to. There are no pending cases and it would appear that the FTC has, from the outset, shown little interest in subliminal advertising as a matter of its legitimate concern.

Sidney Weinstein, President of NeuroCommunication Research Laboratories in Danbury, Connecticut, wrote about the difficulty of enforcing laws against inserting hidden messages in print advertising, particularly. His statement appeared in the June 25, 1984 issue of Ad Age:

> "If such a bill (Wyman's AB-100 in California) could pass the constitutional guarantees of freedom of the press, then the ill-informed, although well-meaning protectors of our vulnerable minds will have an impossible task to perform.

> Consider the watermark present on almost all stationery. To all but the most fastidious examiners of their correspondence, it is the perfect example of a 'subliminal message.' Must every letter contain the disclosure 'Warning: This letter contains a watermark'?

> ...Who will examine with electron microscopes every square millimeter of print ads? Who will perform spectrographic analyses of all audio signals on radio and television commercials? And what objective criteria will this person use to distinguish subliminal messages from random configurations that strike his personal Rorschach fancy?"

Dr. Key, of course, has complained to the FTC on dozens of occasions that he found subliminal SEXes and genitalia, etc. in print and television advertising. On one occasion he paid his own way, from Reno to Washington D.C., to present to the FTC scores of advertisements in which he had found an untold number of male and female body parts, messages, and the ubiquitous "S-E-X."

A small group of FTC attorneys sat through the lengthy session, listening politely and viewing slide after slide of so-called embedded magazine advertisements. There was no discussion afterwards, and the group filed out quietly.

The FTC has, since the ballyhooed birth of the subliminal phenomenon, shown little interest in it. One is led to speculate that its investigators have found subliminals to be but the products of Dr. Key's pathologically glandular imagination.

While the Federal Trade Commission has the primary responsibility for the regulation of advertising in this country, it is the Federal Communications Commission which regulates broadcasting.

And the FCC has declared it "illegal" to use subliminals on the air. Radio and television stations are licensed by the FCC under an assumption that the public owns the airwaves. Radio stations are licensed by the FCC for seven years; television stations for five years. A station, either radio or TV, can lose its license by broadcasting or showing subliminals.

The FCC made its anti-subliminals announcement on January 24, 1974 (FCC 74-78, 29RR 22 395):

> "We believe that use of subliminal perception is not consistent with the obligations of a licensee, and therefore we take this occasion to make clear that broadcasts employing such techniques are contrary to the public interest. Whether effective or not, such broadcasts are intended to be deceptive."

The directive was sent to all broadcasters within a month, interestingly, of the showing of a Christmas TV commercial for a children's game called Husker-Do. The commercial, shown on dozens of television stations, contained a "subliminal " slide "Get It!"

flashed at 1/60th of a second.

The National Association of Broadcasters has also prohibited its members from using subliminals. Its NAB Television code, discarded in 1982, dealt with subliminal messages under its "Special Program Standards" section:

> "Any technique whereby an attempt is made to convey information to the viewer by transmitting messages below the threshold of normal awareness is not permitted."

> 1981 NAB TV Code, IV., 12

The NAB began its TV Code in 1952, using a lot of "shoulds" and "should nots" to loosely guide television executives. The amount of time broadcasters could give advertising was carefully spelled out. The Department of Justice brought suit against the NAB in 1979 for allegedly "artificially curtailing" advertising, repressing price competition, and keeping advertisers from "the benefits of free and open competition." In 1982 NAB signed a consent decree in which it agreed to disband its code-publishing. A federal district court approved the decree.

In England, subliminal messages of any kind are expressly prohibited on radio and television. Interestingly, print advertising remains unrestricted — infest it, if you will, with castrated penises of every length and rigidity — the British courts have, so far, shown an unwillingness to tackle Britain's newspapers, magazines, and billboards.

In Belgium, using subliminals could cost you a year in the slammer and up to 10,000 francs. Belgian legislators enacted the punitive measure in 1972, holding subliminal advertising to be an invasion of privacy:

> "Anyone who by any means whatever projects images or sensations which, though not consciously perceived, are capable of influencing behavior."

> January 26, 1974, Draft Legislation

In Canada restrictions, again, apply only to broadcasters. On

June 27, 1975, the Canadian Radio-Television Commission
(CRTC) (an FCC-like governmental body) issued an amendment to
its Television Broadcasting Regulations:

> "No station or network operator shall knowing-
> ly broadcast any advertising material that makes use
> of any subliminal device. (CRTC 9.1 (1).)

> In subsection (1), 'subliminal device' means a
> technical device that is used to convey or attempt to
> convey a message to a person by means of images or
> sounds of very brief duration or by any other means
> without that person being aware of the substance of
> the message being conveyed or attempted to be con-
> veyed." (CRTC 9.1 (2).)

"It is not illegal in New Zealand," C.R. Ineson, the Executive
Director of the Advertising Agencies' Association of New Zealand
Inc., wrote me in the summer of 1992. "But then again, to my
knowledge no one uses it — mainly because nobody believes it
works."

In fairness, advertising ("commercial speech") has always been a
murky legal area in the United States. Until a couple of decades ago
advertising received no First Amendment protection whatsoever.

In 1976, however, the Supreme Court turned the issue head
over heels in a landmark case involving Virginia Pharmacy vs. the
Virginia Citizens Consumer Council.

The Virginia Citizens Consumer Council, a loose-knit group of
users of prescription drugs in the State of Virginia, brought suit
against the Virginia State Board of Pharmacy and its individual
member pharmacies. They challenged the validity of a Virginia
statute which claimed it was "unprofessional conduct for a licensed
pharmacist to advertise the prices of prescription drugs."

On May 24, 1976 the Supreme Court decided 9-1-1 in favor of
the consumer group.

However, in 1980 the Supreme Court began chipping away at
its 1976 position in a series of cases, declaring the Constitution
"accords a lesser position to commercial speech than to other con-

stitutionally guaranteed expression."

In 1984, as the Supreme Court became more conservative with each passing year, it held that Puerto Rico could ban advertising in Puerto Rico for its gambling casinos, which are legal there. Puerto Rico wanted to continue its casino advertising in the United States, while at the same time discouraging local citizens from patronizing the casinos.

Justice William J. Brennan, Jr. wrote a bitter dissent, claiming that if a product (or activity) is legal, truthful advertising for it should also be legal. He wrote that the majority's opinion would:

> "...dramatically shrink(ing) the scope of the First Amendment protection available to commercial speech and give(ing) government officials unprecedented authority to eviscerate constitutionally protected expression."

With each new case, the Supreme Court seems to be positioning itself for eventually outlawing the advertising of an array of legal products — cigarettes, liquor, contraceptives — for openers. And that, in the words of a 1986 Los Angeles Times editorial, is "inimical to the First Amendment. When it comes to free speech, the justices keep moving in the wrong direction."

Chapter 9

What are we <u>teaching</u> 'em about it?

Chapter 9

What are we <u>teaching</u> 'em about it?

Is the subject of subliminal advertising being raised in the college or university classroom? Specifically in advertising or marketing classrooms? What about classes in other departments?

And what's the instructor telling students about the subject?

Are Americans learning about subliminal advertising from sources outside the classroom? If so, from what sources?

In answer to the first question, a resounding "Yes!" It certainly is being discussed in college and university classrooms. It's a very popular subject. Reinforcement for that remark can be found in some of the professional — and professorial — reaction to my September 17, 1984 cover piece in Advertising Age.

For instance, Charles B. Jones, a Chicago management consultant, found that students in his university guest lectures have been assigned Subliminal Seduction "as required reading." He also asserts that the book "is commonly employed as course reading" in classrooms at other universities as well.

And former Chairman of the board of Ogilvy & Mather, Jock Elliott, claims that "every time we practitioners visit a campus (which is pretty often), we are almost invariably asked about subliminal advertising." Why? Because Dr. Key's been propagandizing pupils "with the blessings of the educational institutions."

Stavros Cosmopulos, well-known Chairman of the Board of Cosmopulos, Crowley, & Daly of Boston claimed that whenever he speaks or lectures in university classrooms "the question of subliminal advertising comes up..."

Yes. Indeed, the subject comes up frequently in college and university classrooms. Professionals know that. And so do educators.

However, we advertising instructors are not promoters of Dr.

Key's threadbare theories. On the contrary. Most advertising educators were at one time, practitioners. Yes, you'll find a few advertising instructors without any full-time professional advertising experience. They are the exceptions. Some support for that view can be found in various studies cited in Billy Ross' annual The Status of Advertising Education. Billy Ross' own study of 135 full-time advertising instructors indicates that the "average" advertising educator has "8 years in advertising."

Nearly all institutions of higher learning mandate several years of full-time professional experience in one's field, along with a Master's or Ph.D. degree, to be considered a viable candidate for a professional track university teaching position.

I know scores of university-level advertising instructors. Yet, I know of only two or three with no full-time previous advertising experience. It invariably comes with the territory. And exceptions are difficult to find.

In 1985 I sampled my advertising teaching colleagues to find out what percentage of them discuss Dr. Key and his whackiness in their advertising classrooms. And how often they brought up his looniness. I was also curious about how they felt about his theories. And how much advertising agency art they thought contained subliminal embeds.

I formulated the questions and a cover letter, and mailed them to the head of each of the thirty accredited university sequences in advertising in the U.S. These are arguably the largest — and perhaps the best — advertising programs in the United States. Each is accredited by The Accrediting Council on Education in Journalism and Mass Communications.

The questions were:

1. Do you, or any other member of your advertising faculty, ever discuss with students in class any of the subliminal advertising theories of Wilson Bryan Key?

2. If you answered 'Yes,' about how often are they discussed?

3. What is your personal feeling about Key's

statement that advertising agencies are constantly and deliberately embedding subliminal words, messages, and even organs of the
body in advertising artwork?

4. What percentage of advertising agency art-
    work, executed for clients, do you feel con-
    tains deliberately embedded subliminal
    words, messages, or organs?

Twenty-two (73%) of the advertising professors responded, and
I reported the findings in a March 4, 1985 Advertising Age.

77% (17) of the advertising instructors who responded reported
that they do, indeed, raise Dr. Key's theories and discuss them in
their advertising classrooms.

Almost two-thirds (65%) of them discuss his accusations every
semester (or quarter).

None of the advertising instructors I polled thought Dr. Key's
statement that "advertising agencies are constantly and deliberately embedding subliminal messages, etc." was believable.

Responses to Question No. 4 brought some mixed signals:

54.5% (12) thought NO agency artwork con-
             tains deliberately embedded sub-
             liminals

31.8% (7)   thought less than 1% of agency
             artwork contains deliberately
             embedded subliminals

9.1% (2)   thought that about 2% of agency
             artwork contains deliberately
             embedded subliminals

4.6% (1)   thought that about 5% of all
             agency artwork contains deliber-
             ately embedded subliminals

100.0% (22)

As I reported in the Ad Age article, many of these advertising educators held very strong opinions about the claims of Dr. Key. Here's a sampling of their views:

> "The subject of subliminal advertising comes up in our Principles of Advertising course each semester. I look forward to the discussion because I take great pleasure in debunking Mr. Key. It amazes me that Key is able to make so much money with statements that have no basis in fact. I worked for 20 years in Chicago advertising agencies and never once did anyone suggest embedding messages in ads."

> "How anyone could ascribe magical persuasive powers to shadows on a shirt sleeve is beyond my wildest imagination."

> "The credibility of Key's work is zero in my view."

> "I agree with you that we as educators must answer our students' concerns about this subject. It is too bad the industry continues its head-in-the-sand posture on the subject, though frankly, I'm not sure what they can do other than taking the subject seriously. We are largely the allies of the industry in trying to reduce the hysteria."

> "You can't avoid discussing the topic. Profs from other disciplines purposely bring it up to our advertising students. We are about the only place on the campus where the students can get an honest answer. I let the book remain on our book list where we can discuss it openly in class. I'd rather the students learn (about subliminals) from me than from others on campus."

> "One has to adopt a strategy of talking (about subliminals) at some length to explain why there's nothing to it."

> "The best thing we can do as educators is answer

questions when they arise as professionally as possible. I'm sure every prof over in Basic Astronomy answers the 'men from other planets' questions in much the same manner."

"One wonders what Key sees in clouds or haystacks or patterned wallpaper. What an imagination."

"I spent 10 years with major advertisers and 10 years with a major advertising agency working with many very large clients. Subliminal advertising was never considered or ever used. I do not believe it exists."

"Occasionally some jerk in an art studio might embed something, but no ad agency would knowingly do so."

"Responsible advertising people don't play games with their clients' money! At least in this country."

"I know of no evidence for viable subliminal advertising use."

Advertising executives are sometimes inclined to brand those of us who teach advertising as "academia nuts," or "irresponsible," "silly," "badly informed," and "misguided." And our painstakingly prepared lectures as "perpetually prurient prattle."

Unlike that view, the replies I received from advertising educators in doing this small piece of research, suggest they have a deep professional concern for their students, and their craft. Their universal approach to the subject suggests a focus that might be labeled industry-oriented.

And, as I stated in the Ad Age piece, "their devotion to their responsibilities suggests they are quite unlike the portrait of the silly and lascivious ad prof painted in the recent parade of letters" (from ad practitioners). (Please see chapter 5).

Their classroom professionalism stands in vivid contrast to Dr.

Key's accusation in Subliminal Seduction that our "so-called educational institutions...have unpardoningly failed to alert us to what
has been going on in the mass media." On the contrary, Dr. Key.

The educators' thoughtful responses to my first question about
discussing subliminal advertising in their college and university
classrooms, convincingly answer his acidic criticism that no marketing or journalism department "...as far as anyone can tell from
the literature, ever introduced the subject into classrooms."

Dr. Eric Zanot's 1983 study of residents of northern Virginia,
Maryland, and the District of Columbia, asked where they had first
learned about subliminal advertising. "Education" was their first
answer, with the greatest number of responses.

But other sources of learning about subliminal advertising were
also important. Of those in his survey who had heard about subliminals, more than half (50.6%) could remember a specific source.
Here's how those respondents recalled learning about subliminal
advertising:

Category	%	(N)
Education	13.5	24
Television	9.6	17
Magazine	6.7	12
Acquaintance	6.7	12
Book	5.1	9
Newspaper	4.5	8
Other	4.5	8
	50.6	90

In the Fall of 1983, Dr. Zanot and Dr. Lynda M. Maddox of
George Washington University reported on their subliminal advertising survey of 199 marketing and advertising professors.
Conscientiously crafted, the study found that all 199 educators had
heard of subliminal advertising. 77% of them — an identical percentage to the number I found in my small study two years later —
devote class time to discussing the phenomenon. And in most cases
the instructor introduces the subject.

Zanot and Maddox concluded that the subject is also discussed in a variety of classes in other departments of a university. Sociology, art, art history, ethics, and psychology come most quickly to mind. Rarely, however, is it discussed in more than one lecture per semester, or quarter.

Similar to my finding was the discovery by Zanot and Maddox that "professors of advertising in journalism or marketing departments teach that subliminal advertising is seldom or never used. When they offer other opinions, they say it is unethical, unacceptable and harmless."

Theodore Schulte, an associate professor in the School of Journalism at the University of Kentucky, finds that about 10% of his beginning advertising students had studied advertising in high school. And that 10% invariably had read one or more of Dr. Key's books. Writing in the April 1, 1985 issue of Ad Age, Professor Schulte chastises high schools for their role in perpetuating the subliminal flimflam:

> "...each year I survey my beginning advertising class to see how many students had any advertising education in high school. Customarily, 10% answer yes. Their books? Their formal introduction to advertising?
>
> Invariably the answer is Subliminal Seduction, Media Sexploitation, The Hidden Persuaders.
>
> They write papers on "Examples of Subliminal Advertising." Nothing here of advertising's role in a free economy, nothing of what advertising does and doesn't do for us, nothing of the lives and work styles of its leaders — just the sensational "subliminal." And this is where this popular idea gets perpetuated, at the high school level. Which points to the desperate need to have some kind of a sane introduction to advertising begin in high school, something which some states, notably Oregon (and soon, we hope, Kentucky) are doing something to correct through local AAF chapters, working with high school programs."

Professor Schulte, a former New York and Chicago copywriter, has a unique way of "handling" the subliminal issue when it arises in his University of Kentucky advertising classroom. He "goes along with it." Agrees that it might exist:

> "Let's suppose art directors and photofinishers all over the country are busy night and day air-brushing sexual images and genitalia into ice cubes, crackers, cereal boxes, bars of soap, products by the millions! Let's say there's a sexual symbol of some kind embedded in illustrations of every product advertised in America.
>
> So what? What's the measurable effect? Do we sell more, even one unit more, of anything because of our carefully contrived sexy subliminals? If so, prove it. (And lots of luck. We have enough trouble trying to prove how advertising works on a conscious level to effect sales, much less worrying about the subliminal.)"

One suspects that Professor Schulte is an excellent teacher. Nice way to make his point.

A Special Thanks

A SPECIAL THANKS

To my wife Therese.

For her encouragement in this project,. And 44 years of unceasing love and support. A very special person.

References

References

References

Adams, Virginia (1982) "'Mommy and I are One' Beaming Messages to Inner Space," Psychology Today (May) pp. 24-26

Anastasi, A. (1964) "Subliminal Perception," Fields of Applied Psychology, A. Anastasi, New York: McGraw-Hill

Baltasar, Gracian y Morales, S.J. (1967) The Art of Worldly Wisdom: A Pocket Oracle, New York: F. Ungar Publishing Co.

Beatty, Sharon E. and Hawkins, Del I. (1989) "Subliminal Stimulation: Some New Data and Interpretation," Journal of Advertising, 18(3), pp. 4-8

Bolen, William H. (1981) Advertising, New York: John Wiley & Sons

Bovee, Courtland L. and Arens, William F. (1992) Comtemporary Advertising, 4th ed., Homewood, IL: Irwin

Brown, J.A.C. (1963) Techniques of Persuasion, Baltimore, MD: Penguin Books

Cuperfain, Ronnie and Clarke, T.K. (1985) "A New Perspective of Subliminal Perception," Journal of Advertising, 14(1), pp. 20-24

Dudley, Sid C. (1987) "Subliminal Advertising: What is the Controversey About?" Akron Business and Economic Review, 18 (Summer) pp. 6-18

Dunn, Watson S. et al (1990) Advertising: Its Role in Modern Marketing, 7th ed., Hinsdale, IL: The Dryden Press

Engel, Jack (1980) Advertising: The Process and Practice, New York: McGraw-Hill

Etc.Etc.Etc., A Publication of the American Society of Advertising and Promotion, Inc. (1990) "Subliminals: Marketing Hopes and Fears," (April) pp. 1-3

Fox, Stephen (1984) The Mirror Makers, New York: William Morrow and Company, Inc.

Gable, Myron et al (1987) "An Evaluation of Subliminally Embedded Sexual Stimuli in Graphics," Journal of Advertising, 16 (1) pp. 26-31

Gable, Myron et al (1987) "Effect of Subliminal Stimuli on Consumer Behavior: Negative Evidence," Perceptual & Motor Skills (December) 40(3) pp. 847-854

George, Stephen G., Jennings, Luther B. (1975) "Effect of Subliminal Stimuli on Consumer Behavior: Negative Evidence," Perceptual and Motor Skills (December) 40(3) pp. 847-854

Goldiamond, I. (1966) "Statement on Subliminal Advertising," Control of Human Behavior, Vol. 1, Glenview, IL: Scott Foresman

Goldman, Debra (1992) "By The Book," Adweek, May 18, p. 16

Goodis, Jerry (1979) "Help! There's Sex In My Soup: A Small Plea for an end to Subliminal Silliness," Quest, Feb.-Mar.

Haber, Ralph Norman (1959) "Public Attitudes Regarding Subliminal Advertising," Public Opinion Quarterly, 23, pp. 291-293

Haberstroh, Jack (1984) "Subliminal ads: Threat or hoax?" Advertising Age, 55 (September 17) pp. 3, 42, 47

——(1985) "Ad professors deliver subliminal education," Advertising Age, 56 (March 4) p. 52

——(1985) "Fevered Fantasies, Wilson Bryan Key just won't go away," London Magazine (March) pp. 17, 18, 23

——(1985) "To tell the truth: Subliminal seduction," Research in Action, 9 (Spring) pp. 10-14

Harris, R.J. et al (1979) "Learning to Identify Deceptive Truth in Advertising," Current Issues and Research in Advertising, U. of Michigan Graduate School of Business Administration, Division of

Research, Ann Arbor

Hawkins, Del. (1970) "The Effects of Subliminal Stimulation on Drive Level and Brand Preference," Journal of Marketing Research, 8 (August), pp. 322-326

Hovsepian, A. and Quatman, G. (1978) "Effects of Subliminal Stimulation on Masculinity-Femininity Ratings of a Male Model," Perceptual and Motor Skills, 46 (February), pp. 155-161

Jewler, A. Jerome (1985) Creative Strategy in Advertising, Belmont, CA: Wadsworth Publishing Company

Kanner, Bernice (1989) "From the Subliminal to the Ridiculous," New York Magazine (December 4) pp. 18-20

Kelly, J. Steven (1979) "Subliminal Embeds in Print Advertising: A Challenge to Advertising Ethics," Journal of Advertising, 8 (Summer) pp. 20-24

Key, Wilson B. (1973) Subliminal Seduction, New York: Signet

———— (1976) Media Sexploitation, New York: Signet

———— (1980) The Clam-Plate Orgy, New York: Signet

———— (1989) The Age of Manipulation, New York: Henry Holt and Co.

Kiesel, Diane (1984) "Subliminal Seduction: Old Ideas, New Worries," American Bar Association Journal, 70 (July) pp. 25-27

Kilbourne, William E. et al (1985) "The Effect of Sexual Embedding on Responses to Magazine Advertisements," Journal of Advertising, 14, No. 2, pp. 48-56

Krajick, Kevin (1990) "Sound Too Food to Be True?" Newsweek, (July 30) pp. 60-61

Los Angeles Times (1986) Editorial: "Free Speech Gets Fuzzier," Part II (July 4) p. 4

Mandel, Maurice (1968) Advertising, Englewood Cliffs, NJ:

Prentice-Hall

Moore, T.E. (1982) "Subliminal Advertising: What You See Is What You Get," Journal of Marketing, 46 pp. 38-47

—— (1988) "The Case Against Subliminal Manipulation," Psychology & Marketing, Vol. 5(4) (Winter), pp. 297-316

Morse, Robert C., Stoller, David (1982) "The Hidden Message That Breaks Habit," Science Digest, 90(9) (September) p. 28

McConnell, J.V. et al (1958) "Subliminal Stimulation: An Overview," American Psychologist, 13 (No. 3) pp. 229-242

McDaniel, Stephen et al (1982/83) "Subliminal Stimulation as a Marketing Tool," The Mid-Atlantic Journal of Business, 20(1) (Winter) pp. 41-48

McKerracher, Keith (1985) "Subliminal Advertising: Modern Day Myth," The 4A's Washington Newsletter, Feb-March, pp. 6,8

Nelson, Roy Paul (1989) The Design of Advertising (6th ed.), Dubuque, IA: Wm. C. Brown Publishers

Nieves, Evelyn (1989) "Unlocking mind's power," Middletown, NY, Times Herald Record (March 28) p. 29

Ogilvy, David (1992) "We sell. Or else." The Advertiser, 3 (Summer) pp. 21-25

O'Toole, John (1989) "Those sexy ice cubes are back," Advertising Age, 60 (October 2) p. 26

Packard, Vance (1957) The Hidden Persuaders, New York: Pocket Books

Patti, Charles H., Frazer, Charles F. (1988) Advertising: A Decision-Making Approach, Hinsdale, IL: The Dryden Press

Pratkanis, Anthony, Aronson, Elliot (1992) Age of Propaganda, New York: W.H. Freeman and Company

—— and Greenwald, Anthony (1988) "Recent Perspectives on

Unconscious Processing: Still No Marketing Applications," Psychology & Marketing, 5(4) (Winter) pp. 337-350

Rogers, Martha and Smith, Kirk H., (1993) "Public Perceptions of Subliminal Advertising," Journal of Advertising Research (Mar./April) pp. 10-18

Rogers, Stuart (1993) "How a Publicity Blitz Created the Myth of Subliminal Advertising," Public Relations Quarterly (Winter) pp. 12-17

Ross, Billy I. (1991) The Status of Advertising Education, Lubbock, TX: PrinTech

Runyon, Kenneth E. (1984) Advertising (2nd ed.), Columbus, OH: Charles E. Merrill Publishing Co.

—— (1979) Advertising and the Practice of Marketing, Columbus, OH: Charles E. Merrill Publishing Co.

Saegert, Joel (1979) "Another Look at Subliminal Perception," Journal of Advertising Research, 19 (February) pp. 55-57

—— (1987) "Why Marketing Should Quit Giving Subliminal Advertising the Benefit of the Doubt," Psychology & Marketing, 4 (Summer) pp. 107-120

Schulte, Theodore (1985) "Getting to the underlying truth on subliminal ads," Advertising Age, 56 (April 1) p. 28

Severance, L.J., Dyer, F.N. (1973) "Failure of Subliminal Word Presentations to Generate Interference to Color Naming," Journal of Experimental Psychology, 101 (1) pp. 186-189

Sharp, Heber C. (1959) "Effect of Subliminal Cues on Test Results," Journal of Applied Psychology, 43 (6) pp. 369-371

Silverman, Lloyd H. (1976) "Psychoanalytic Theory: 'The Reports of My Death are Greatly Exaggerated,'" American Psychologist, 31 (September) pp. 621-637

—— and Weinberger, J. (1985) "Mommy and I are One: Implications for Psychotherapy," American Psychologist, 40, pp.

1296-1308

Synodinos, Nicolaos E. (1988) "Subliminal Stimulation: What Does the Public Think About It?" Current Issues & Research in Advertising, Vol. 11, Nos. 1 and 2, pp. 157-187

Time Magazine (1979) "Secret Voices," (September 10) Vol. 114 (11) p. 71

Trachtenberg, Jeffrey A. (1987) "Beyond the hidden persuaders," Forbes (March 23) Vol. v139n6, pp. 134-136

Viewpoint (1984) "Editorial: Scrutinizing 'Subliminal' Ads," Advertising Age, 55 (September 24) p. 18

——— (1984) "Letters," Advertising Age, 55 (October 8) p. 22

——— (1984) "Letters," Advertising Age, 55 (October 22) p. 22

——— (1984) "Letters," Advertising Age, 55 (November 5) p. 24

——— (1984) "Letters," Advertising Age, 55 (December 3) p. 20

Vokey, John R., Read, J. Don (1985) "Subliminal Messages: Between the Devil and the Media," American Psychologist (November) 40(11) pp. 1231-1239

Weinstein, Sidney (1984) "Beware Subliminal Laws," Advertising Age, 55 (June 25) pp. 20-21

——— et al (1986) "Effects of Subliminal Cues in Print Advertising upon Brain Response, Purchase Intention, and Simulated Purchase," Advertising and Consumer Psychology, 3, pp. 3-16

Weir, Walter (1992) How to Create Interest-Evoking, Sales-Inducing, Non-Irritating Advertising, Binghamton, NY: The Haworth Press

——— (1984) "Another look at subliminal 'facts,'" Advertising Age, 55 (October 15) p. 46

Wells, William et al (1989) Advertising: Principles and Practice, Englewood Cliffs, NJ: Prentice Hall

Wright, R. (1973) "The Cognitive Processes Mediating Acceptance of Advertising," Journal of Marketing Research, 10 (February) pp. 53-62

Zanot, Eric J. et al (1983) "Public Perceptions of Subliminal Advertising," Journal of Advertising, 12(1) pp. 39-44

—— and Maddox, Lynda M. (1983) "Subliminal Advertising and Education," Journal of Marketing Education, (Fall) pp. 13-17

Zuckerman, M. (1960) "The Effects of Subliminal and Supraliminal Suggestions on Verbal Productivity," Journal of Abnormal and Social Personality, 60(3) pp. 404-411

About the author

Dr. Jack Haberstroh

About the Author:

Dr. Jack Haberstroh is an Associate Professor of Advertising in the School of Mass Communications at Virginia Commonwealth University in Richmond.

He spent more than seventeen full-time professional years in advertising and publication management. He's owned several businesses, including two small newspapers in the Long Beach, California area.

Dr. Haberstroh received his Ph.D. in Mass Communications from the University of Iowa in 1969, and has been teaching advertising at the university level ever since. Eight years at San Diego State University, the last nine at VCU.

He is the author of an advertising copywriting workbook, Copywriting Assignments from America's Best Advertising Copywriters (1989) Prentice Hall. As this volume goes to press, two other books of his are under publication review.

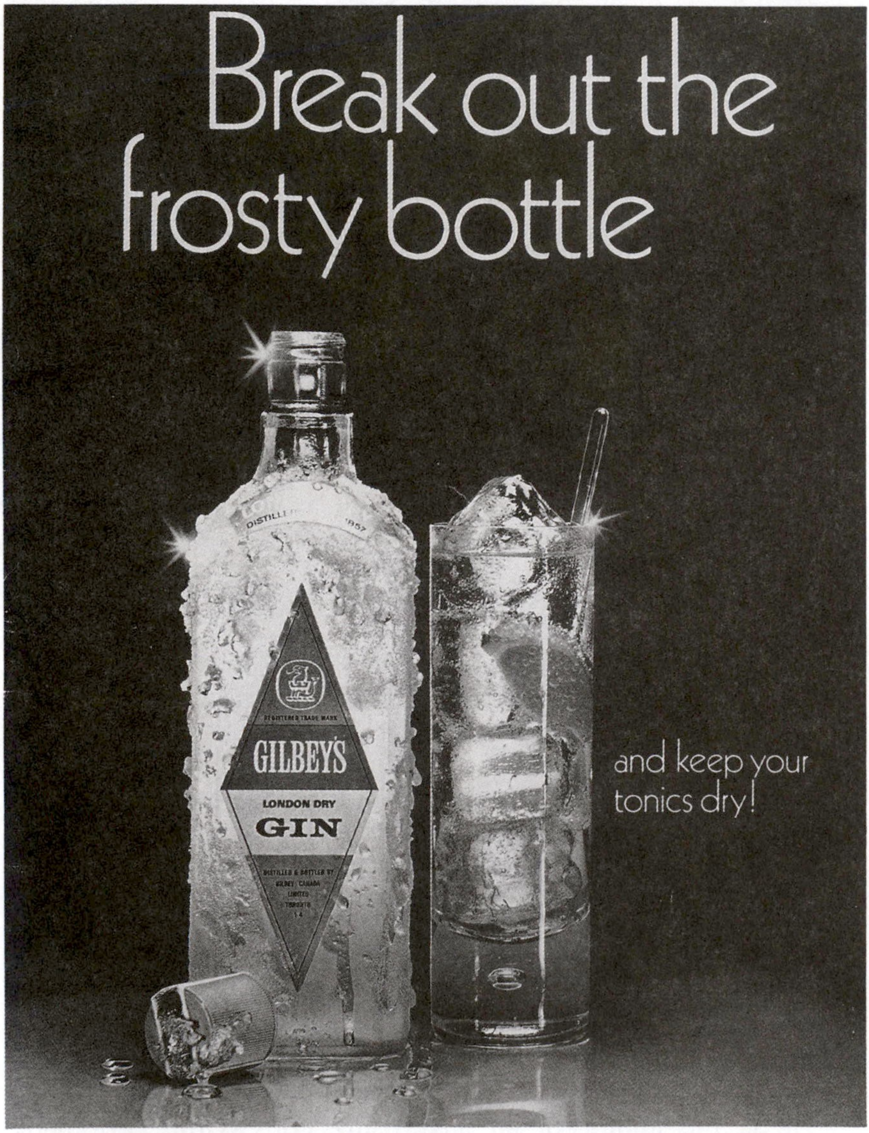

Fig. 1

Fig. 2

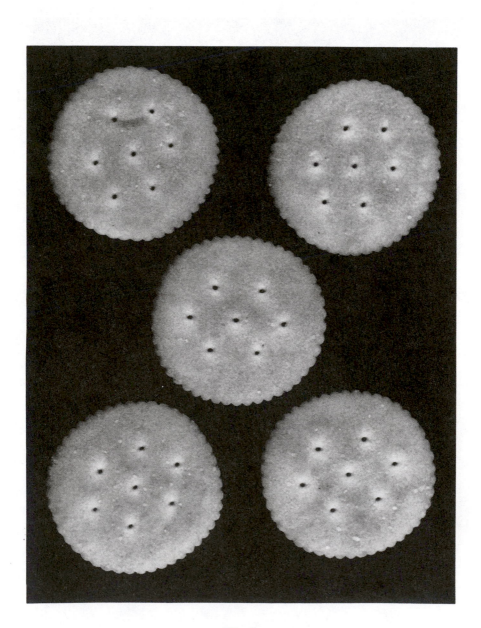

Fig. 3

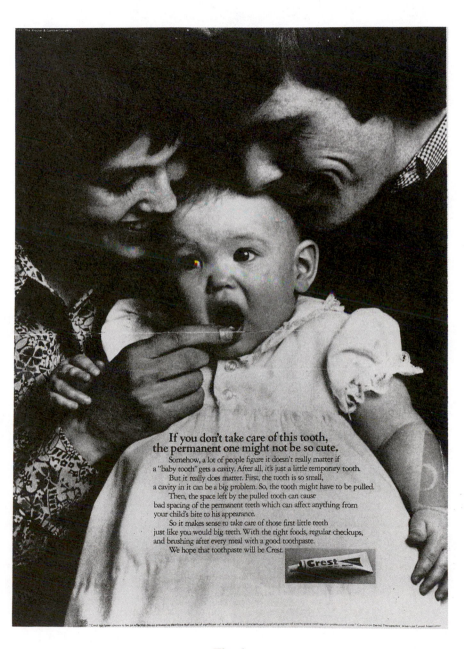

Fig. 4

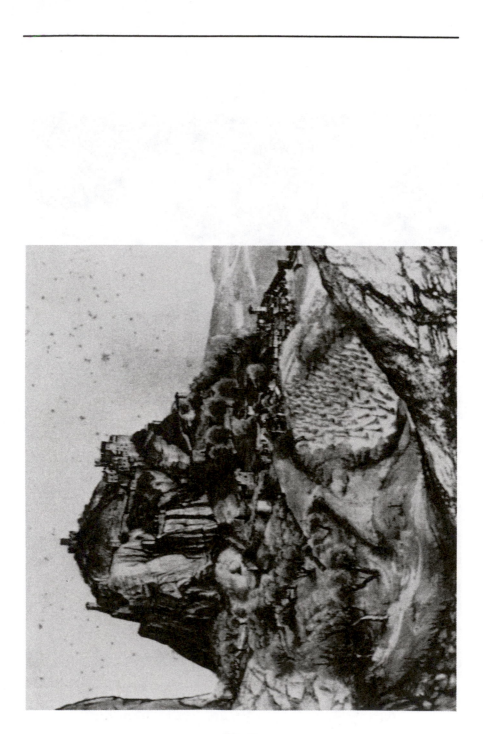

Fig. 5

Fig. 6

Fig. 7

Fig. 8

Fig. 9

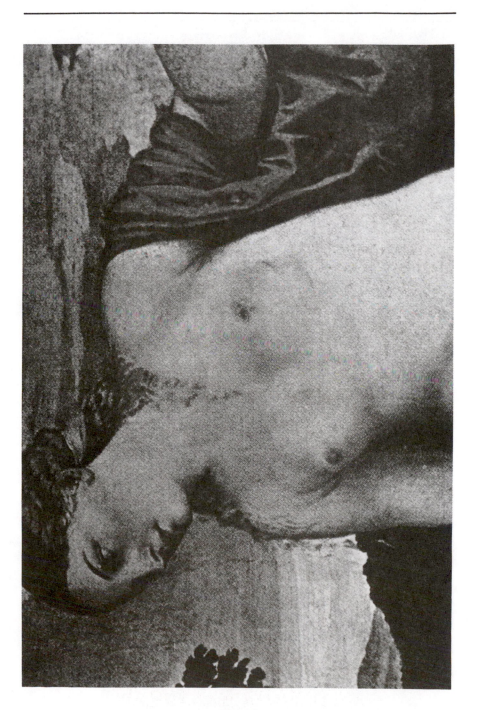

Fig. 10

Fig. 11

Fig. 12

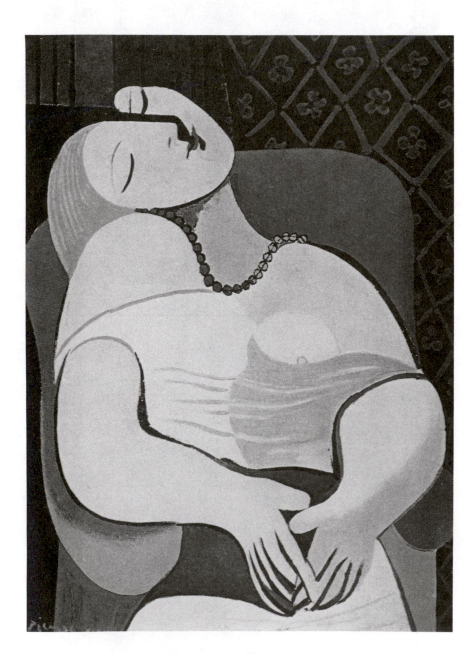

Fig. 13

PEOPLE HAVE BEEN TRYING TO FIND THE BREASTS IN THESE ICE CUBES SINCE 1957.

The advertising industry is sometimes charged with sneaking seductive little pictures into ads.

Supposedly, these pictures can get you to buy a product without your even seeing them.

Consider the photograph above. According to some people, there's a pair of female breasts hidden in the patterns of light refracted by the ice cubes.

Well, if you really searched you probably *could* see the breasts. For that matter, you could also see Millard Fillmore, a stuffed pork chop and a 1946 Dodge.

The point is that so-called "subliminal advertising" simply doesn't exist. Overactive imaginations, however, most certainly do.

So if anyone claims to see breasts in that drink up there, they aren't in the ice cubes.

They're in the eye of the beholder.

ADVERTISING
ANOTHER WORD FOR FREEDOM OF CHOICE.
American Association of Advertising Agencies

Fig. 14

Fig. 15

BACARDI light rum. Its subtle flavor makes it perfect for daiquiris, the Bacardi Cocktail, martinis, or with fruit juices, soda or tonic. Use Bacardi light rather than gin or vodka. *Daiquiri recipe:* Squeeze ½ lime or lemon. Add ½ teaspoon sugar, jigger of Bacardi, ice. Shake and serve. (Or use a daiquiri mix.) For the Bacardi Cocktail, add a teaspoon of grenadine.

BACARDI dark rum. Slightly more pronounced in flavor, yet smooth and mellow. Best for highballs, sours, rum & colas, Manhattans, eggnog, on-the-rocks, with water, hot rum drinks or any mixer. Use Bacardi dark rather than whiskey.
BACARDI 151. A very high proof rum. Enjoy it in exotic drinks like the Mai-Tai, in hot rum drinks, gourmet cooking and dramatic flaming dishes.

AÑEJO™. The world's smoothest liquor? Quite possibly. Añejo is the ultimate rum. It's been delicately aged. So it is very dry and mellow. In fact, many connoisseurs prefer it to brandy. Sip it from a snifter. Enjoy it in a highball or on-the-rocks. Magnifico.

BACARDI® rum-the mixable one

Which Bacardi for what?

Fig. 16

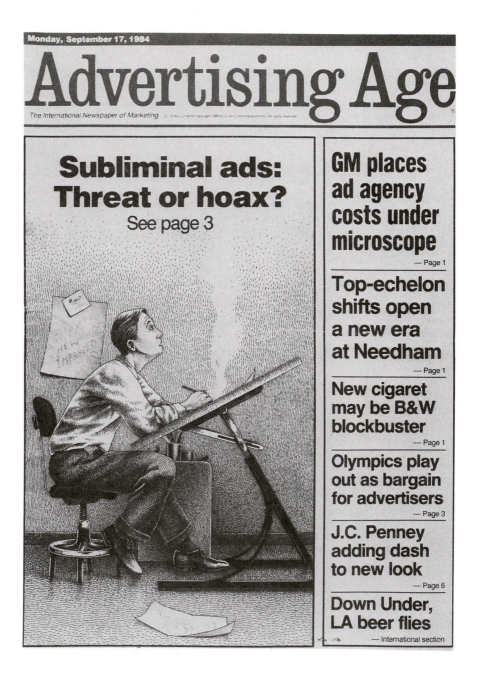

Fig. 17

Fig. 18

Fig. 19

Fig. 20